∞

Unbelief

Fr. Nicolas J. Laforet

Unbelief

∞

Its Causes and Cure

Revised, enlarged, and edited by
James Cardinal Gibbons

SOPHIA INSTITUTE PRESS
Manchester, New Hampshire

Unbelief: Its Causes and Cure comprises part 2 of *Why Men Do Not Believe* (New York, 1909; a translation of *Pourquoi l'on ne croit pas* [Louvain, 1864]). This abridgment of the whole book has been edited slightly to eliminate anachronisms and other anomalies. Unfortunately, the author did not always provide readers with information about persons mentioned or sources quoted. Where possible and appropriate, we have identified them, leaving intact the author's notes where better information could not be found.

Cover design by Perceptions Design Studio.

On the cover: Lighting flare (125975474) Copyright © 21 / Shutterstock.com.

Scripture passages in this book are taken from the Douay-Rheims Version of the Bible.

Sophia Institute Press
Box 5284, Manchester, NH 03108
1-800-888-9344

www.SophiaInstitute.com

Sophia Institute Press® is a registered trademark of Sophia Institute.

Library of Congress Cataloging-in-Publication Data

Names: Laforet, Nicolas Joseph, 1823-1872, author.
Title: Unbelief : its causes and cure / by Fr. Nicolas J. Laforet ; revised, enlarged, and edited by Cardinal Gibbons.
Other titles: Why men do not believe
Description: Manchester, New Hampshire : Sophia Institute Press, 2017. | Originally published under title: Why men do not believe, 1869.
Identifiers: LCCN 2016050684 | ISBN 9781622823963 (pbk. : alk. paper)
Subjects: LCSH: Apologetics. | Christianity and atheism. | Atheism. | Skepticism. | Irreligion.
Classification: LCC BT1212 .L3413 2017 | DDC 202 — dc23 LC record available at https://lccn.loc.gov/2016050684

First printing

Contents

∞

Preface

It is useless to deny that in Christian communities many men are to be found who no longer believe in Christianity. Many even, not content with rejecting the religion of Jesus Christ, go on to deny God; or if they do not deny Him in express terms, their idea of Him is radically false, and they seek to place upon the altar of the living God, the Creator of heaven and earth, a philosophical idol, ten thousand times vainer than the idols of wood and stone to which pagan nations offered incense.

Whence comes this infidelity?

According to those who pride themselves on being philosophers or critics, the denial of Christianity, or even of a personal and living God, is dictated by science and reason; it is, they say, the natural and legitimate fruit of intellectual progress; rationalists, spiritualists, materialists, atheists, pantheists, skeptics of every kind all alike appeal to science and reason to justify their belief or their doubts in the eyes of the public, and even apparently to their own conscience.

I willingly bear this testimony to learned unbelievers of every shade, that they can shelter their infidelity under the finest and noblest pretexts. I have no intention here to examine or discuss

Unbelief

those scientific and philosophical pretexts that they call decisive and unanswerable reasons. This has been done elsewhere,[1] and Catholic writers continue to do so daily with the authority that belongs to true learning. I am going to attempt another method.

I have often reflected, sometimes with wonder, always with sadness, on the phenomenon of infidelity in the midst of the light of Christianity. I have frequently asked myself, in the sincerity of my heart, why so many men — many of whom are noble-minded, serious, learned — reject the teaching of the Catholic Church, the organ and representative of our Lord Jesus Christ upon earth — why certain minds, rather than submit to the authority of the Church, will descend to a total denial of the moral and religious order, and even to universal doubt. In this fact there is certainly matter for psychological and moral study of high importance and melancholy interest.

I know very well that in the eyes of infidels this fact appears the simplest and most natural thing in the world. I know that they affect to place their infidelity under the direct and exclusive patronage of science and philosophy. But I am convinced that science and philosophy are in no way interested in the hostile or indifferent attitude that they assume toward the Christian Faith.

Christians have always possessed, and still, thank God, possess, as large a measure of science and philosophy as infidels. Infidelity depends on other causes. What these causes are I propose now to make the object of my inquiry. I cannot hope to bring to light all the real causes of infidelity. There are some that necessarily escape the eye of the observer, however attentive he may

---

[1] See James Gibbons, *The Faith of Our Fathers: Being a Plain Exposition and Vindication of the Church Founded by Our Lord Jesus Christ.*

Preface

be. There are mysteries in the depths of the human soul that the eye of God alone can penetrate. But it is easy for anyone who has had an opportunity of closely observing believers and unbelievers, and of studying their history, to recognize the principal and ordinary causes of infidelity.

In the first part, after a few words on the preaching of Jesus Christ, and the opposite effects produced by it, we shall mark, by a few examples, the principal phases of the twofold history of the Christian Faith, and of unbelief in the bosom of Christianity. This history will afford us valuable lessons; it will show us how men become, how they remain, and how they cease to be Christians. We shall see, by the experience of eighteen centuries of the human mind, whether the source of infidelity can possibly be the development of reason and the progress of intelligence.

In the second part, relying on the lessons of history and on psychological and moral observation, we shall seek to unfold the real causes of religious unbelief. We shall begin by defining the nature of faith and the nature of infidelity; we shall then analyze the principal forms of contemporary infidelity, and we shall seek to distinguish the diverse and often complex conditions of the soul, to which they attach themselves, or by which they are produced.

We trust that God will make use of these pages, humble though they be, to confirm some souls in the happy possession of the Faith, and to rescue others from the corroding bitterness of doubt, or from the gloomy, icy void of unbelief, leading them back to the bright and sweet repose that Christian Faith alone can give.

∞

Notice to the Second Edition

This book has already produced consoling fruits. God has used it as His instrument to bring back many wandering souls to Christian faith and practice.

The Sovereign Pontiff, Pope Pius IX, had foretold this result in a letter addressed to the author a few weeks after the publication of this work. We give a translation of this letter.

Letter of Pope Pius IX

Illustrious and Reverend Sir:

To the more considerable works which you have already published you have added one which, though small in size, will, as its title promises, prove of the greatest utility. For, as in the art of healing the body its diseases are treated with the greatest ease and security when their true cause is known, so may the maladies of the soul be best and most effectually resisted and cured when their origin has been ascertained. As the plague of unbelief, which is the principal evil of our day, proceeds either from corruption of heart, or from the languor of religious feeling, or from the madness of pride, to discover such causes and to bring them to light by tearing from them the veil under which they disguise their shameful deformity will assuredly be a powerful aid to souls, helping them reject error and gain free access to truth.

Therefore, our most Holy Father especially approves its design, and has charged me to return to you his thanks and to assure you from him that he foresees most abundant fruit from the labor which you have undertaken, and, as a pledge of that success, to convey to you his Apostolic Benediction, which he gives you with the tenderest affection.

Having had the pleasure of fulfilling this agreeable task, I offer you also the expression of my particular respect and esteem, and pray God to bestow all his favors upon you.

Your most humble and devoted servant,
Franciscus Mercurelli
Secretary to His Holiness, Pope Pius IX

∞

Foreword

We who possess the light of divine faith should not censure too severely those who are deprived of that sublime gift. We should rather assist them by prayer and by trying to lead them to a better way of thinking. They are not the only ones to blame. The three great enemies of man's salvation—the world, the flesh, and the devil—have much to do with unbelief: "All that is in the world is the concupiscence of the flesh, and the concupiscence of the eyes, and the pride of life, which is not of the Father, but is of the world."[2]

This evil of unbelief is deeply seated; it is largely traceable to the corruption of human nature: "The earth was corrupted before God, and was filled with iniquity."[3] We are a fallen race. Mankind fell from the favor of God by the disobedience of our first parents in transgressing the commandment of their Maker. Since that day the natural tendency of human nature is toward evil: "The imagination and thought of man's heart are prone to

[2] 1 John 2:16.
[3] Gen. 6:11.

evil from his youth."[4] We see this principle in the repugnance of children to obey their parents; in the tendency of some citizens to rebel against law, order, and authority. Hence, on account of this corrupt nature, we see the inclination of some persons toward dishonesty, and of others toward anger, revenge, impurity, and so forth.

In any indulgence of this kind, corrupt nature imagines that it sees and enjoys a good. Whatever stands in the way of the enjoyment of that apparent good seems to corrupted nature to be an evil. On this principle, parents seem to be an evil standing in the way of disobedient children; the police force and sheriff, who are the friends and protectors of good citizens, seem to be an evil to the shoplifter, the lascivious street walker, and the keepers of houses of ill fame. On the same principle, God, in whom the good Christian sees a Friend, a Father, and a Benefactor, seems to be an evil to the impure and the wicked.

Now, the wayward child, by his bad reasoning, desires to get his parents out of the way, or to be removed from their influence. The disorderly citizen and the train robber, by their unwarranted reasoning, would like to see the police and the sheriff meet with defeat or destruction, because these officials stand in the way of their unruly desires.

By the same process of bad reasoning the impure and the wicked desire to strike a deadly blow at God Himself and to deny His rights and even His very existence, because God and His rights and His commandments stand in the way of their bad lives.

This is the main principle underlying much of the unbelief and infidelity of the present day: "Men loved darkness rather than the light, for their works were evil. For every one that doth

---

[4] Gen. 8:21.

evil hateth the light, and cometh not to the light, that his works may not be reproved."[5]

In the Beatitudes our Lord tells us: "Blessed are the clean of heart, for they shall see God."[6] The unclean of heart do not perceive the ways of God, His providence, His goodness, His conditions of salvation; for, as St. Paul reminds us, "The sensual man perceiveth not these things that are of the Spirit of God; for it is foolishness to him, and he cannot understand, because it is spiritually examined."[7]

These principles will be developed in the following pages.

—James Cardinal Gibbons

---

[5] John 3:19–20.
[6] Matt. 5:8.
[7] 1 Cor. 2:14.

∞

Unbelief

1

∞

What Faith Is

Many people have a strange idea of religious faith. Some look upon it as only an office of the imagination, or, at most, of the feelings. According to them religion is wholly in the emotional part of the soul; reason has nothing to do with it. Hence they consider all religions as indifferent in themselves. Religious feeling may be produced under diverse forms. These forms are of no importance; it is sufficient that the feeling be sincere, and that it show itself by the homage of a respectful submission to the Divinity. The question of doctrine and truth wholly disappears; it is of no moment to know whether a religious belief be true or false, if it be conformable or contrary to reason; all is judged exclusively from the point of view of the heart.

This is truly a senseless opinion, insulting alike to reason and to God. Yet a great number of men hold it, according to whom Christian faith is a blind sentiment, more or less respectable, that may be good enough for the common people but is unworthy of a cultivated mind guided by the light of reason.

On the other hand, men are to be found who place themselves at a wholly opposite point of view; who persuade themselves that faith is the work of the understanding alone, that feeling and the will have no part in it. And they conclude thence that faith is not free, that it in no way depends on us, and that if some receive the Christian creed while others reject it, it is because they see, or think they see, what is hidden from the others. If it were so, unbelief could never be a sin; at most, putting things at their worst, it would be only a mistake. Men who reason thus can have reflected but little on the part the will plays in the adhesion of the soul to truth.

Let us begin by recalling the principles of Catholic theology on the nature of faith. When these principles are known, it will be easier to discern the causes of infidelity. It is necessary to know exactly what the Christian Faith is in order that we may comprehend what the obstacles are that hinder its birth and growth in a soul, that we may know what things are most likely to weaken or even extinguish it in a soul where it already exists.

To believe, in the religious and Christian sense of the word, is to adhere to any truth on the authority of God, who is the revealer of that truth. Human faith accepts a thing on the testimony of man; divine and Christian faith on the testimony of God. We believe all the articles of the Catholic creed because we are convinced that all these articles have been revealed by God, and consequently they have for their warrant the testimony of God Himself. We do not adhere to such or such a doctrine as the object of our faith, on the word of the pope, or of the Church. In our eyes the Church is but a means of going to God, a medium divinely established to communicate the teaching of God to us. The Church is not the truth; she is its guardian and its organ; she bears witness to the truth.

We must observe, by the way, that the Catholic Church and the divine revelation made in Jesus Christ are two things absolutely inseparable. From the moment we admit that God has made a divine and supernatural revelation to the human race, and that He has prescribed a religion for men to follow, we must also necessarily admit that His providence has established an authority charged to maintain this religion pure and entire, to preserve it, and to propagate it.

It is absurd, supremely absurd, to suppose that God would reveal and establish the religion that men must follow in order to attain their end, and then leave this religion to itself, abandon it to chance, without any care for its fate, suffering it to become corrupt and to fade away by contact with time, and the interested caprices and innumerable moral and intellectual weaknesses that human nature continually displays. A God who could act thus could not be to us a personal God, infinitely wise and perfect; He would be a being as inexplicable as the god of Epicurus, a god whom reason must disown.

Many Protestant authors, in spite of their prejudices, recognize the necessary and indissoluble union between Christian revelation and the Church. "When we start from a supernatural principle in religion," says Staeudlin, "we must necessarily admit that the Divinity, who has deigned to make this revelation to man, must have taken care that it should not be abandoned to the arbitrary judgment of men; not to admit this principle is to argue inconsistently."[8] "What the doctrine of Divine Providence is with regard to the creation," says another Protestant writer, "such is the doctrine of the infallibility of the Church with regard to Divine Revelation. They must stand or fall together."[9]

The Divine Word, which the Church does but repeat and explain to men, cannot deceive. God is Truth, and the Truth does

---

[8] *Staeudlin's Magazine*, vol. 3, p. 83.
[9] *N. Quartalschrift*, Jahrgang 9, no. 3.

not lie. When it is once thoroughly established that a doctrine comes from God, it would be absurd to demand other proofs of the truth of this doctrine. People do not ask Truth if it speaks the truth. Our Faith, resting on the authority of the Divine Word, is therefore sheltered from all error; the foundation on which it rests is immovable. It is supremely reasonable, for it depends on the veracity of God Himself, who is infinite reason.

We are certain that the doctrines to which we adhere by divine Catholic Faith really come from God. We do not admit lightly or without cause the fact of divine revelation; we believe it on the authority of truths whose evidence in our eyes is absolutely incontestable and twenty times more striking than that which surrounds the best authenticated historical facts.

These proofs form what is called in theology *motives of credibility*. These are the preliminaries of faith—preliminaries that human reason has a right to demand and may examine by the light of earnest, upright, loyal criticism. Christianity does not fear an attentive and thorough examination of its title deeds. On the contrary, it calls for it.

But people must not deceive themselves. However evident the motives of credibility may be in themselves, they do not suffice to produce faith in the soul; they prepare the way for faith, but they do not create it. The causes on which faith depends are higher, and of a more interior nature. Here we must strive to understand thoroughly the teaching of Catholic theology, throwing light, as it does, upon depths whose existence is not even suspected by multitudes of inattentive and superficial minds.

St. Thomas Aquinas gives the following definition of faith: "To believe is an act of the understanding adhering to divine truth by command of the will, which is moved by the grace of God. The act of faith is subject to free will in relation with God, and therefore it is meritorious."[10] We shall make a brief commentary on this definition, in which all is comprised. Faith is the result of the combined action of God and man. Let us see first what man does; then we will show what he receives from God, and how far he must be aided by God in order to believe with a supernatural and true faith.

The understanding does not act alone in man in the formation of the act of faith, but the will also, and principally; it is the act of the whole soul, with all its faculties, all its powers. To believe is assuredly, as St. Thomas says, an act of the understanding, because the object of faith is divine truth, and truth in itself is the object of the understanding and not of the will. The understanding is made to know that which is true; the will is made to love and conform itself to that which is good. It is therefore exact to say that faith is the direct and immediate act of the understanding, not of the will.

But it is only by the intervention of the will, which moves, directs and commands it, that the understanding accepts divine truth and gives adhesion and assent to it. There is no constraint upon the will with regard to the direction it shall take, and in which it will be followed by the understanding: the will is free. Undoubtedly it can, under grave responsibility, choose between two contrary directions and, consequently, either unite and bind the understanding to truth, or turn it away, and precipitate it into error. On this account, the act of faith, on the firm adhesion of the understanding to divine truth, is meritorious. It is a free act, free with a liberty subject to trial, and not yet fixed in the love and possession of the truth. Suárez justly observes that, to accomplish the act of faith, it is not sufficient that there

---

[10] Thomas Aquinas, *Summa Theologica*, II-II, Q. 2, art. 9.

be no repugnance in the will to believe; it is necessary that by a positive act it move the understanding to attach itself to revealed truth.[11]

It is, then, the will that is the principal agent of faith in us. It is not the understanding, but the will, that decides with regard to faith. In order to believe we must will to believe—will it positively and seriously. The direction and assent of the understanding depend upon the will. In this sense St. Augustine says, and St. Thomas repeats after him, that faith dwells in the will of those who believe: "Fides consistit in credentium voluntate."[12]

I fear that this doctrine, which gives so great a preponderance to the will in the act of faith, may astonish and disturb more than one of my readers who are accustomed to look only to the understanding when the knowledge and acceptance of truth are in question. But they may be reassured. I am confident that if they will read to the end, they will see that the principles of Catholic theology on the adherence of the soul to divine truth are in harmony with the fundamental and intimate laws of our nature, and can be misunderstood only by a prodigiously superficial psychology. I will confine myself for the present to some short remarks.

Most theologians, in explaining the free and meritorious character of the act of faith, content themselves with observing

> that the object of faith is obscure to us, not evident in itself. Thus the dogmas of the Holy Trinity, of the Incarnation, of the Redemption, of the Eucharist, for example, are certainly not in themselves evident to our reason;

---

[11] Francisco Suárez, *De Fide*, disp. 6, sect. 6, no. 7.
[12] Thomas Aquinas, *Summa Theologica*, II-II, Q. 5, art. 2.

they are mysteries; that is to say, obscure truths superior to reason, truths in which sober minds will always find sufficient explanation to believe, and never as much as is needed to comprehend.[13]

The proofs that bear testimony to the existence of divine revelation are evident—they ought to be evident; they are the motives of credibility—but the things revealed, being above reason, remain obscure; not wholly obscure, doubtless, for in that case they could not be known, and faith would be impossible, but in that kind of half-obscurity that excludes evidence. This defect of evidence, as theologians justly remark, explains the possibility of hesitation and denial on the part of the understanding and shows the necessity of the preponderance given to the will in the accomplishment of the act of faith.

This is elementary to anyone who reflects. The mind, not being subjugated by evidence, may accept or reject the truth that is offered to it; all depends on the disposition of the will.

But we must go further. Supposing the truths proposed were not superior to reason, a sad and daily experience shows that reason might still reject them. Liberty plays a considerable part even in the domain of truths of the natural order, on which the clearness of rational evidence sheds light.

Is not the existence of God evident? And yet men are to be found—I mean learned men, men of cultivated minds—who are ignorant of God, or who form so unnatural a notion of him that the God whom they seem to acknowledge presents none of the features of the living and true God.

---

[13] Gottfried Wilhelm Leibniz, *Discours de la Conformité de la Foi Avec la Raison*, no. 56.

Unbelief

What is more evident than the freedom and immortality of the soul? And yet these truths meet with contradiction, and obstinate contradiction.

Whence comes this? Do not these facts offer abundant proof that the assent of the mind remains free, even in the face of evidence? How could it be free if the will—the sole power in us that is free—did not intervene in the judgments we form?

We must not forget that our understanding is not a solitary faculty, living and acting by itself alone in entire independence. It is closely united to the other powers of our soul and is moved and governed by the will, the center and chief of these powers. The will makes the man in the moral and religious order, as it does in the social order; and it exercises an incalculable power even in the order that appears purely intellectual. I shall return to this subject hereafter.

Let us now show, according to Catholic teaching, what part is necessarily borne by God in the act of faith.

"To believe," says St. Thomas, "depends on the will of those who believe; but the will of man must be prepared by God through grace, and thus be raised to the supernatural order."[14] Faith appertains to the supernatural order; hence it cannot be the work of nature, nor of our soul abandoned to its own strength. Let us hear on this point the second Council of Orange, whose decisions have been received as rules of faith throughout the whole Catholic Church:

> If anyone shall say that by the powers of nature we can do any good in order to attain the salvation of eternal life—that we can think or choose as we ought, or consent

---

[14] Thomas Aquinas, *Summa Theologica*, II-II, Q. 6, art. 1, ad. 3.

to the preaching of salvation, that is to say, to the Gospel—without the light and inspiration of the Holy Spirit (who gives to all the sweetness which makes us consent to and believe the truth), such a one is seduced by the spirit of heresy, and hears not the voice of God, which says in the Gospel, "Without me you can do nothing" (John 15:5).[15]

If anyone shall say that the beginning as well as the increase of faith, and even the pious sentiment by which we believe in him who justifies the ungodly, and attain the new birth of holy baptism, is in us naturally, and not by the gift of grace, that is to say, by the inspiration of the Holy Spirit, which corrects our will, and turns it from infidelity to faith, from impiety to piety—such a one shows himself opposed to the apostolic dogma, the blessed Paul saying, "Being confident that he who hath begun a good work in you will perfect it unto the day of Christ Jesus" (Phil. 1:6); and elsewhere, "Unto you it is given for Christ, not only to believe in him, but also to suffer for him" (Phil. 1:29); and, "For by grace you are saved through faith, and that not of yourselves, for it is the gift of God (Eph. 2:8)."[16]

These decisions of the Council of Orange were confirmed by Pope Boniface II. In the letter that the pontiff wrote on this subject to the illustrious Saint Cesarius of Aries, who had presided over the council, we read:

We rejoice greatly that in the Council which you and certain Bishops of Gaul have held, the Catholic Faith

---

[15] Council of Orange, chap. 7.
[16] Ibid., chap. 5.

has been followed, in defining by common consent, as you point out, that the faith by which we believe in Jesus Christ is given to us by Divine Grace correcting us.... For it is a certain and Catholic dogma, that in all good works, of which faith is the chief, even before we have yet willed, Divine Mercy rectifies us, in order that we may will; it accompanies us when we will, and follows us in order that we may persevere in the faith.[17]

Grace must therefore rectify our will, and incline us to consent to, and to believe revealed truth; it must accompany and sustain our changeable and inconsistent will in this holy disposition; finally, it must follow the goodwill it has inspired and help us to will to adhere always to the Word of God.

Nothing in the principles of Christianity can be simpler or more logical than this doctrine. We are not created for a purely natural end, one to be realized by the mere exercise of our natural powers, but for a supernatural end, above the reach of our faculties. This end is to see God face-to-face, or in His essence, as He is in Himself, a single nature subsisting in three distinct persons; to possess Him fully, and to enjoy the happiness attached to such possession.

This vision of God, this beatitude, is manifestly above nature. How can we attain it? The happiness of a free and intelligent being consists in the realization of his end, and he must achieve it by his own acts; but the acts of man, in themselves, are not means proportioned to an end superior to nature. In order, therefore, that there may be harmony or proportion between

---

[17] Philippe Labbé, *Sacrosancta Concilia ad Regiam Editionem Exacta*, bk. 4.

the means and the end, it is necessary that these acts should be elevated, ennobled, transformed, by a principle superior to nature, and thus become supernatural; this principle is grace. Is it not a common axiom that means must be proportioned to their end? If, then, the end of man is supernatural, his acts, which are the means by which he must attain this end, must of necessity be supernatural, and consequently animated by a principle superior to nature. This reasoning appears to me geometrically exact.

Grace, by which God enlightens our understanding with a supernatural light, attracts, fortifies, and elevates our will, sows in us the seed of that higher life that is to become the Christian life, and will be the initiation and first faint sketch of that eternal life, which begins upon earth and will be finished and consummated in the glory of heaven. "Grace and glory," says St. Thomas, "are generically one; because grace is nothing else than a certain beginning of glory in us."[18]

Now, faith is precisely the beginning of that supernatural life, of which the glory of the beatific vision will be but the marvelous completion. It is by faith that man enters of full right, if I may thus speak, in the supernatural order. It is, therefore, easy to understand the indispensable necessity of grace for the act of faith.

There are three kinds of life possible to man in this world:

1. the life of the body or of the senses

2. the life of mere natural reason

3. the life of grace, raised above nature by faith, and working by charity

---

[18] Thomas Aquinas, *Summa Theologica*, II-II, Q. 24, art. 3, ad. 2.

Unbelief

"The first," says a religious writer, whose simple, frank language I will venture to borrow, "is the life of an animal; the second, the life of a man; the third, the life of a Christian." This author adds:

> The carnal man, the man wholly immersed in the animal life—a drunkard, for example—can conceive nothing beyond eating and drinking, nothing beyond the body and what flatters the senses. All that is intellectual—science, poetry, moral beauty—all is folly to him. The rationalist or philosopher, wholly taken up with nature, can conceive nothing above human reason. All that is supernatural and divine faith and grace is folly to him. He is to the Christian what the drunkard is to the philosopher. The carnal man may mistake or deny the intellectual order: that order, none the less, exists. In the same way the rationalist may mistake or deny the supernatural order, the order of grace: that order, none the less, exists. The carnal man, who would raise himself to the intellectual order, must in some sort die to himself in order to enter a new state of existence, a new world. The rationalist who would raise himself to the supernatural order, the order of grace and faith, is obliged in some sort to die to himself, in order to enter a new state of existence, a new world such as he had never even suspected. The carnal man in becoming a rational man ceases not to be a man, but becomes better and nobler. The rational man in becoming a man of faith ceases not to be a rational man, but becomes a man of Divine reason.[19]

Rationalism recognizes only the first two of these states—life according to the senses and life according to reason; it altogether

---

[19] René François Rohrbacher, *De la Grâce et de la Nature*, 32, 40.

denies the supernatural life, the life of faith. Such a denial is precisely as well founded as that of the animal man, who denies the life of reason because it is extinct in him. Maine de Biran, after having traversed all the phases of rationalism, came to discern clearly these three states of existence in man, by simply psychological observation; and with the exception of a few inaccuracies of language, unavoidable in one who is a stranger to theological study, he has described them well.

He names these three conditions of life: the animal life, the human life, the spiritual life.

Whatever blind philosophy may say, faith does not destroy nor lower reason, but, on the contrary, strengthens and raises it in a singular degree. Did faith lower the reason of St. Augustine, St. Thomas, Leibniz, Bossuet, Joseph Görres? Faith gives to human reason a superior light that, at the same time that it reveals absolutely new horizons to our gaze, illuminates with a clearer and brighter light the domain that the eyes of our understanding have already discerned. Philosophers who reject faith to confine themselves to mere reason are just like astronomers who would lay aside the telescope to study the heavens with their naked eye. Faith is the telescope of human reason. Armed with this powerful help our understanding has a clearer conception of that which is within its reach and in the heaven of heavens, beyond its natural horizon. It discovers new and marvelous worlds, to which its unaided vision could never have attained. To reject faith is manifestly to diminish reason, and to deprive it of its most wonderful auxiliary to knowledge.

Faith, inasmuch as it is light, produces a twofold effect in us: first, it reveals to us truths of the supernatural order; next, it adds to the truths in the natural order already discerned by reason (such as the existence of God, His attributes, the Creation of the world, providence, the spiritual nature, liberty, and immortality of the soul).

More than this, faith, as light and as power, purifies the eye of the understanding from a thousand foreign elements that embarrass it and hinder its free exercise. It gives a movement to the will that turns it toward God and the intelligible world, and at the same time raises the whole soul, helps it to shake off the yoke of those things that are inferior to its nature, and leads it toward those higher regions in which its destiny calls it to move and live. Faith is a power that struggles against the inclination, unhappily innate in fallen man, that drags our soul toward inferior objects and imparts to us a contrary inclination. Plato would say that faith restores to the human soul the wings that were broken in its fall.

From the Catholic dogma that grace is necessary to enable us to believe with a divine supernatural faith, let no one infer that there are therefore men necessarily condemned to be without faith, because God has not given them the grace to believe. The Church, which knows God and beholds in him a compassionate Father, and not an unjust master gathering where he has not sown, teaches that He refuses grace to none. It is also Catholic dogma that God wills all men to be saved, and that He offers to all the grace necessary to enable them to acquire the ineffable glory to which He bids them. The Council of Trent declares that "God commands nothing impossible; when he orders anything, he at the same time warns us to do what we can, to ask for what we cannot do of ourselves, and he will help us to do it."[20]

To ask for what we are unable to attain of ourselves is the ordinary condition that God imposes for the bestowing of His favors. He wills that we, who are created and essentially dependent

---

[20] Council of Trent, sess. 6, chap. 11.

beings, should confess our own insufficiency and implore the aid of him from whom light and strength descend. The old man who showed forth the teaching of the gospel to the philosopher Justin when he was seeking for the truth, said to him, "Pray that the gates of light may be opened before you; for no one can see and comprehend these things unless God and his Christ give him understanding."[21] Justin followed this counsel and was rewarded by a faith that he sealed with his blood. If men who do not believe would pray as this ardent and generous philosopher prayed, they would, I am convinced, soon believe with a faith as firm as his.

---

[21] Justin, *Dialogue with Trypho*, chap. 7.

2

∞

The Nature of Unbelief

Infidelity is the opposite of faith. Generally speaking, we call anyone an infidel or unbeliever who does not bend his reason before divine revelation and submit to its authority. Infidelity is the denial of all divine revelation—of the primitive revelation made to the father of the human race, continued later to the patriarchs, then to the prophets of God's people, and finally accomplished in Jesus Christ, the Author and Finisher of our Faith. Unbelief denies the supernatural order and the miraculous order that supposes and involves a divine revelation. It denies any determinate and positive intervention of God in the history of humanity. It absolutely ignores the immense divine fact that occupies the two epochs of history—the epoch of the ages anterior to Jesus Christ, and the epoch of the ages that followed Him—the fact that shines with incomparable brilliancy in Christian society, the most moral, learned, civilized, powerful society that the world has ever seen.

The infidel pretends to rely solely upon reason; he admits no other light than the natural light; he recognizes no other facts than those that can be explained by natural causes; miracles in his eyes are a chimera as much as divine revelation; he rejects all that surpasses the power of nature, as well as all that exceeds the light of reason.

Such is the general character of infidelity as it shows and asserts itself in the midst of Christian Europe. All our unbelievers, to whatever school they belong, and however great may be their differences, agree in the denial of the supernatural and the miraculous; all make a boast of recognizing only reason and nature. Therefore, the names of naturalism and rationalism express exactly the common principle that unites them.

St. Thomas teaches that infidelity, like faith, is an act of the understanding, but an act commanded by the will. He says, "Infidelity, as well as faith, is in the understanding as in its immediate subject; but it is in the will as in its first mover." He adds: "It is the contempt of the will which causes the dissent of the understanding, and it is in this dissent that infidelity essentially consists. Hence the cause of infidelity is in the will, although infidelity itself is in the understanding."[22] Infidelity, having its cause in the will, is, like faith, a free act; it is the fruit of a free decision of the mind. Therefore, it is imputable. "Faith is a virtue, and infidelity is a vice."[23]

It is scarcely necessary to observe that it does not follow from hence that every man who does not believe in the Christian revelation is necessarily guilty. A man may be unbelieving and yet not an infidel in the strict sense of the word. Infidelity, properly so called, as St. Thomas defines it, supposes that the ignorance of divine revelation is not wholly involuntary. There are men who do not know, and who, morally speaking, cannot know, Jesus Christ. Therefore, these men do not believe in Him, but their

---

[22] Thomas Aquinas, *Summa Theologica*, Q. 10, art. 2.
[23] Ibid., Q. 10, art. 1.

infidelity is a purely negative infidelity, as St. Thomas calls it. They are nonbelievers rather than infidels; this absence of faith is not imputable to them because it is nowise in their will. There is no real, and consequently no culpable, infidelity, in the theological sense of the word, except voluntary infidelity.

Where there is no freedom, there is no sin: this is an elementary principle of morals. But there is another principle no less elementary that is too often forgotten, and it is this: a thing may be voluntary directly or indirectly, in itself or in the cause on which it depends. God alone knows the secret dispositions of the soul, and the obstacles that many unbelievers oppose, more or less voluntarily, to faith. It is indisputable that the will plays an important part in infidelity, and this will be better understood as we proceed.

The diverse forms of rationalism, which are but different degrees of infidelity, would suffice to justify the doctrine of St. Thomas on the first and fundamental cause of unbelief. All unbelievers affirm, with marvelous unanimity, that they will obey reason and reason alone; they add, with one voice, that the language of reason is sufficiently clear on all questions that affect the destiny of man, and that they need no other teacher.

If it be thus, whence arise those radical differences that divide the faithful and respectful disciples of reason into two opposite camps? Whence comes it that Renan, an atheist and materialist, contradicts on all the principles of morality Jules Simon, who, like him, recognizes no other authority than reason? Is it not because all do not equally listen to the voice of reason, whose sovereignty they proclaim in theory while they ignore and resist it in fact?

How many men assume toward reason the same attitude that the best of the rationalists assume toward faith! The sophists, by an evil and culpable disposition of the will, ignore the authority of reason, as the rationalists ignore the authority of faith.

There are rebels and revolutionists in the kingdom of reason as there are in the kingdom of faith. There are also, which is sometimes more excusable, sick and languishing minds whom the light wounds and who see things only through a deceptive medium. This intellectual malady has too often a voluntary cause; but sometimes it is the result of education and circumstances from which its victims have been unable to free themselves.

In the first half of this century pantheism reckoned the greatest number of celebrated followers; now materialism is regaining favor and is received and supported by many learned unbelievers. Evidently neither pantheists nor materialists follow the natural light of reason; they are in open revolt against it, declared rebels to its authority. Spiritualistic rationalism looks upon them in this light as we do.

There are also among our infidels skeptics who no longer believe in any certainty, and who, despairing to find truth, close their eyes and bury themselves in a factitious slumber that completes the ruin of their understanding. They are sick and imagine they will find health and rest in suicide.

Spiritualistic rationalism is certainly the most reasonable form of infidelity; but its most distinguished representatives act with regard to the motives of credibility of the Christian Faith (which are as evident as the freedom and immortality of the soul) in the same way that skeptics, materialists, and pantheists act with regard to the evident truths of reason. I am aware of the fine pretexts with which they cloak their unbelief; but are not they themselves also aware of the pretexts with which the miserable

crowd of sophists cover their daring negations? Let them lay
aside pretexts: let them go to the bottom of things and, with
their hand on their conscience, dare to ask themselves seriously
and sincerely why they do not believe.

3

∞

Science Is Not the Cause of Unbelief

Before pointing out in detail the real causes of unbelief, we will glance at the pretext ordinarily employed by men of all kinds who reject the Christian Faith. All, whether skeptics, atheists, pantheists, or spiritualistic rationalists, pretend that our belief, which was perhaps good for unenlightened ages, cannot bear critical investigation by the human mind; reason goes beyond it; science exposes its failings and errors.

Certainly it is strange to see a religion that has been at the head of civilization for eighteen centuries, and whose creed has been accepted, defended, and glorified by the most eminent intellects and most illustrious philosophers, from St. Justin to Lacordaire and Joseph Görres, condemned with such self-sufficiency and, we may add, with such levity. Will anyone dare to say that there has ever been a society equal to the Christian society for power of reasoning and extent of knowledge? I protest that I can with difficulty regard the proud anti-Christian declarations of contemporary unbelief in a serious light, and were it not that charity for human souls obliges me to bear with the most unreasonable prejudices, I would be tempted to answer them only by contemptuous silence. But it is the duty of the disciples and ministers of Jesus Christ to compassionate all the intellectual and moral infirmities of their brethren.

It is unnecessary here to examine and discuss directly the motives of the nonacceptance that rationalism opposes, in the name of philosophy and science, to the teaching of the Christian Faith; this has been done elsewhere.[24] We will recall only a few contemporary facts, which, in our opinion, demonstrate that infidelity has nothing in common with scientific progress.

In the early ages of Christianity, pagan philosophers ridiculed the simplicity of Christians and represented them as the enemies of reason, philosophy, and science. Celsus and Porphyry, not to mention other names, attacked the gospel upon principles similar to those that rationalism now employs. But these attacks did not hinder philosophers and learned men of the first order, such as St. Justin, Athenagoras, Tertullian, Clement of Alexandria, Arnobius, and St. Augustine, from bowing their reason before the authority of the gospel and submitting their understandings to the Christian Faith. Who, in these days, speaks of the criticisms of Celsus or Porphyry?

And since a new paganism has sought to raise its head in Europe, the same phenomenon is reproduced before our eyes. While a certain number of men denounce the Christian Faith as the antithesis of philosophy and science, men of eminent minds are to be met with, who, having passed the greater part of their lives in infidelity, returned to this Faith and proclaim that all the objections of rationalism, which had so long held them back, have no pretensions to science and rest upon prejudices unworthy of an earnest mind. This is a fact of the highest

[24] See Henry F. Brownson, *Faith and Science; or, How Revelation Agrees with Reason, and Assists It.*

importance, which would alone suffice to show the puerility of infidel pretensions.

Since the beginning of this century, how many learned men have been seen to desert the standard of rationalism and range themselves under the banner of the Faith! Nor can it be said of these learned converts, as it is said of us, that in their profession of the Faith they do but obey the prejudices of education; for on entering the Church they have been obliged to break with their past life, and often with habits of mind contracted since the first real dawn of reason. Who will dare to say that men such as Frederick Schlegel, Maine de Biran, Lherminier, Augustin Thierry, and many more as learned as they were strangers to the progress of modern criticism or deficient in intellectual independence?

We will pause at only two names, Augustin Thierry and Maine de Biran, of whom one represents historical, and the other philosophical criticism.

Augustin Thierry claims a place in the first ranks of the restorers of historical research in France. No one, in the annals of literature, presents a more wonderful example of perseverance in labor and devotion to science, even for years after he went blind. "For thirty years," says Father Gratry, the friend and confidant of the illustrious historian,

> it was the will of God to shroud this luminous understanding in material darkness, and imprison this energetic will in a motionless body. But the soul confined in this prison, and wearing this chain, continued its work and its persevering search after God and his truth.... Perfectly blind, entirely paralyzed, instead of giving way to heaviness and dullness, he watched, meditated, listened, and dictated; and with what brilliancy, what enthusiasm! His life was

regulated and disciplined by the inflexible exactness of an almost religious rule.

This energetic and unconquerable mind entered on the study of history with the most hostile prepossessions against the Christian Faith, and he often evinced great injustice toward the Church. But what was the result of his researches and meditations? It was the profound conviction that all the philosophical and historical difficulties of which unbelief makes so much are but phantoms that fade away as soon as they are exposed to the light of serious examination. Let us hear Father Gratry:

Having abandoned infidelity, as he himself has often told me, he soon learned from the sincere study of men and of history that infidelity does not explain the mystery of the world, and that the living power which leads mankind is religion. History further showed him that this religion can be no other than Christianity. But as his mind rose by degrees from error to truth, he thought at first to have found the pure doctrine of the Gospel in Protestantism. At that time, he sought for light at Geneva.

"Then [these are his own words] I had no notion of the history of the Church. When I had cast my eyes over it, I saw clearly that Protestantism could not be the religion founded by Jesus Christ. Protestantism and history are wholly incompatible. The Protestant system has been forced to construct a fictitious history for its own use. I am astonished that people can still maintain themselves on such ground. How is it that they do not see that Catholicism is found entire in the first four centuries?" Another day, quite recently, he said to one of the Fathers of the Oratory, M. Pinaud: "People sometimes maintain — and it is a prejudice I shared for a long time—that the doctrine of the Church is formed of pieces and fragments. How false this is! What admirable unity we find in her teaching! The examination of the text soon overthrows this error."

In the rationalist world, in the midst of which Augustin Thierry had passed his life, people wondered that so many learned men should be converted to Catholicism and submit the reason they had so long held in independence to the authority of the Church.

A week before his death this learned and conscientious man spoke of this fact to Father Gratry:

> Many persons cannot understand how it happens, or whence it comes, that so many should return to the Catholic Church in spite of objections and difficulties. It is very simple: it is because Catholicism is the Truth. It is the true religion of mankind. Pretended philosophical objections are not philosophical; on the contrary, all the philosophy of all times and all places is found in the Catholic Doctrine. All truth centers in it, and men plunge into falsehood in proportion as they wander from it.
>
> This is why Lutheranism is worth less than Anglicanism, Calvinism less than Lutheranism, Unitarianism less than Calvinism, and so of the rest.
>
> On the other hand, I see no good reason against the Catholic Religion. If we consider the precepts of the Church, they are good, reasonable, salutary, even to the smallest practice: none can be omitted without leaving cause for regret. People do wrong to hesitate. They must

come thither at last. True philosophy, true practical wisdom will be sure to lead men thither.

Many false judgments, many religious errors, are to be found in the works of Augustin Thierry. He had intended to correct all that he had written against the truth. Death surprised him in the midst of these generous labors. He said to Father Gratry: "I wish to correct all that I may have written, although in good faith, against the Truth, anywise. Every day and every night I implore God to give me time to finish this work, for it seems to me that in this I am working for God. I am often sustained and encouraged in my weariness and sleeplessness by this thought: I am God's workman. But do not repeat this," said he, with delicate modesty, "it would be presumptuous. I only say it to you."

"If I am not deceived," says Father Gratry in conclusion, "this example will become historical; it will be salutary to many; it will raise many from despair; it will cure the blindness of many." Certainly it is well calculated to dispel prejudices, and to raise up weak and wavering minds.

The conversion of Maine de Biran is not less striking than that of Augustin Thierry. Cousin said of this philosopher that he was "the greatest metaphysician who had adorned France since Malebranche." We should not exaggerate: Maine de Biran is not a great metaphysician; he does not come near Malebranche; but he is an eminent psychologist, and undoubtedly one of the most sagacious and profound observers known to the philosophy of the present century.

How could a man who had Condillac for his master, and who has not studied in the school of Plato and St. Augustine, become a metaphysician? Maine de Biran, like all his unbelieving contemporaries, began with the philosophy of sensation and the degradation of materialism. How long a road he had to travel before he could reach the heights of Christian Faith! He did travel this road slowly, painfully; and by force of perseverance and courage he triumphed over the obstacles of every kind that he met with on this long journey.

The serious observation of the phenomena of thought and the activity of the ego soon showed Biran how empty was the philosophy of sensation. Materialism was vanquished, but the philosopher did not dream of replacing it by Christianity. He remained an infidel for a long time. The morality of stoicism pleased his noble and generous soul, and he would have declared himself the disciple of Zeno had not the feeling of reality, always so vivid in him, shown him the chimerical side of this proud philosophy. His ideas with regard to the nature of religion were most false. He wrote thus in 1815: "Religion is a sentiment of the soul, rather than a belief of the mind; in it, belief is subordinate to feeling." This is exactly the inverse of the truth. At the same period, he gave an account of the state of his soul and of the intellectual freedom with which he pursued the search after truth:

> In my youth, and when I was prepossessed in favor of the materialistic systems which had seduced my imagination, I put aside all ideas which did not tend to this end. I was frivolous rather than insincere. But since my own ideas have led me far from these systems, I have had no prepossession in favor of any fixed conclusion at which I would arrive, no prepossession either in favor of belief or of unbelief. If I find God and the true laws of the moral order, it will be by good fortune, and I shall be more worthy of credit than they who, with so many prejudices, tend only to establish them by their theory.

Unbelief

Alas! this mind, which believed itself so free, obeyed unwittingly a multitude of prejudices fostered by anti-Christian ignorance. Three years later, this philosopher, till then so proud of his reason and moral strength, experienced an invincible need of leaning on God.

I leant on myself, I reckoned on my faculties, I hoped that they would continually develop, I expected great progress from time and labor; experience teaches me that I leant upon a feeble reed, agitated by the winds, broken by the tempest. Our faculties change and deceive our expectations; we have as little ground to believe in their power and duration as in their authority. When a man seeks not God, he doth himself more harm than the whole world and all his enemies can do him.

This last sentence is taken from the *Following of Christ*. At the time when Biran wrote these lines, he was continually reading that incomparable book. The *Pensées de Pascal* and Fénelon's *Oeuvres Spirituelles* were of the number of his favorite works. He tells us that in 1815 he was in the habit of beginning each day by reading a chapter of Holy Scripture. This acquaintance with the doctrines revealed by God completed and corrected that work in his soul that his own moral and psychological experience had begun.

As it happens almost always with earnest rationalists, this man, formerly so proud, so confident in his powers of reason and will, came scarcely to believe either in one or the other; he had fallen into a kind of moral and intellectual depression.

Men begin with senseless pride, and end with despair, because they obstinately reject all support but self, that poor, feeble reed that bends and breaks so easily. But in this sad state of weakness,

Biran happily turned toward God and asked for light and strength from Him who is the Truth and the Life.

He prayed.

When a soul prays, it is saved. We cannot too often repeat what reason and history agree in attesting, that prayer is the key of faith. When a man humbly confesses his own insufficiency and sincerely asks God to enlighten and strengthen him, he is very near believing and being a Christian.

Listen to Maine de Biran, to whom, a little while back, religion was but a matter of feeling, and Christian mysteries but dreams and chimeras:

> Religious and moral belief, which reason does not originate, but which forms a basis and necessary starting-point of departure for reason, is now my sole refuge; and I find true science precisely there, where formerly, with the philosophers, I saw only dreams and chimeras.

"Religion alone solves the problems proposed by philosophy." "The help of God," adds this undeceived rationalist,

> is necessary for us even in those things which are, or appear to be, in our own power. I find myself stripped of all my faculties precisely because I relied too much on myself, and had not acquired the habit of confiding in the assistance of a superior power and asking for it by prayer, in order that I might be strengthened.

> There are three very different kinds of disposition of the mind and soul: the first, which is that of most men, consists in living exclusively in the world of phenomena (that is to say, the world of business, pleasure, glory), and taking them for realities. Hence arise inconstancy, disgust,

perpetual change. The second is that of reflective minds who long for truth in themselves and in nature by separating appearances from realities, and who, finding no fixed basis for this truth, in despair fall into skepticism. Finally, the third is that of souls enlightened by the light of Religion, which alone is true and immutable. They alone have found a sure support; they are strong because they believe.... The greatest benefit Religion has bestowed upon us is the saving us from doubt and uncertainty, which are the greatest torment of the human mind, the true poison of life. In a mind destitute of religious belief all is undetermined, fugitive, and changeable.

The human mind is not made to walk alone; it walks securely only when leaning on Divine Authority. It hesitates and totters even in the domain where it is naturally intended to move, unless sustained by the hand of God. Maine de Biran had observed this fact of daily experience in himself and in the society in which he lived. We rarely meet with infidels, even among the best, who firmly and constantly adhere to the truths of natural religion.

In the state in which man is born, he has need of the grace of God for two ends. First, he has need of a medicinal grace to cure the wounds of his nature and to fortify his understanding and his will, so as to enable them, as Fénelon says, to attain their end (*aller au bout d'elles-mêmes*).[25] Maine de Biran saw perfectly the necessity of this grace; perhaps, as usually happens with minds that have relied too much on themselves and have been cruelly

---

[25] This expression, rather trivial in its form, may be rendered: "To go as far as they are capable of going themselves."

deceived, he exaggerated the extent of this necessity. Secondly, man has need of grace to raise himself to the supernatural order, which is, properly, the order of faith, as we have already explained. Even before he fully embraced the Faith, our philosopher had clearly perceived the reality of this supernatural order, and the necessity of grace to attain it and maintain himself in it. No psychologist has ever more clearly seen what rationalism obstinately denies, that man is called to live a life superior to the life of the senses and of mere reason; that our nature, such as God has made it, calls for this life, but that it is not possible without supernatural help, which is grace. Let us hear this scrupulous and profound observer of the human soul:

> There are not only two opposing principles in man, there are three; for there are three kinds of life and three orders of faculties. If there were perfect accordance and harmony between the sensitive and active faculties which constitute man, there would still be a superior nature — a third life which would not be satisfied, and which would make us feel that there is another happiness, another wisdom, another perfection beyond the greatest human happiness, the highest wisdom and intellectual and moral perfection of which a human being is susceptible.[26]

In the last pages of this *Journal Intime*, Biran returns continually to these three kinds of life: the life of the senses, the life of pure reason, and the super-rational life, or the life of faith; he has made the distinction between these three kinds of life one basis of his *Nouveaux Essais d'Anthropologie*. This superior life

---

[26] Pierre Maine de Biran, *Journal Intime*, 399.

is instilled into us by the Spirit of God, which acts in us and communicates with our soul without being confounded with it.

> The delusion of philosophy is to consider the principle of spiritual life as exclusively belonging to the ego, and because our ego can to a certain point free itself from dependence on sensible objects, to look upon it as independent of that other superior influence whence it receives all that light which it does not originate.... I was formerly puzzled to understand how the Spirit of Truth could be in us without being ourselves, without identifying itself with our own spirit, our ego. Now I comprehend the interior communication of a Spirit superior to us, which speaks to us, which we hear within us, which vivifies and fertilizes our spirit without being confounded with it.... This communication of the Spirit with our spirit when we know how to call him to us, or to prepare for him a fit dwelling within us, is not only of faith, it is a veritable psychological fact.
>
> The whole doctrine of Christianity is comprised in love. When we have felt within ourselves the vivifying influence of the Divine Spirit, it is natural that we should love him, that we should invoke him without ceasing, as the food, support, principle of our life; that we should love him more than ourselves, for from him we hold an existence superior to that of self, and it is by love alone that we unite ourselves to the Spirit.[27]

Rationalism denies this action of the Spirit of God in us, and the life that that action inspires and nourishes; but this denial,

[27] Ibid., 405, 10, 11.

contradicted moreover by the principles of true philosophy, cannot prevail against a fact that all Christians experience, any more than the denial of a blind man would prevail against the fact that there is light, which all whose eyes are open see.

It is impossible [again says Maine de Biran] to deny to the true believer who experiences in himself what he calls the effects of grace; who finds the repose and peace of his soul in the intervention of certain ideas or intellectual acts of faith, hope, and love; and who is thence able to satisfy his mind with regard to problems which no other system can solve; it is impossible, I say, to dispute what he experiences, and consequently not to recognize the true foundation there is in him, or in his religious belief, for those conditions of soul which constitute his consolation and his happiness.[28]

The following lines are the last that occur in the *Journal Intime* of Maine de Biran, and they deserve the attention of all men who think themselves strong enough to walk alone, and who proudly repulse the hand that God offers them by His Son Jesus Christ:

There should always be two, and we may say of man, even the individual man, *vae soli*! If a man is carried away by the unruly affections which absorb him, he can form no just judgment either of outward objects or of himself; if he abandon himself to them, he is unhappy and degraded, *vae soli*! A man may be ever so strong in reasoning powers and in human wisdom, but unless he feel himself sustained

---

[28] Ibid., 405.

by a power and reason higher than himself, he will be unhappy; he may impose on others, he cannot impose on himself. True strength, true wisdom consists in walking in the presence of God, and in feeling his supporting hand, otherwise *vae soli!* The stoic is either alone, or with the belief in his own strength, which deceives him; the Christian walks in the presence of God and with God, by the Mediator whom he has taken for the guide and companion of his present and future life.

These lines, the truth of which every sincere and upright mind will attest, were penned by Maine de Biran on the seventeenth of May 1824. Two months later he died, with sentiments of lively faith, consoled and fortified by the presence of our Divine Mediator, who came to visit him in the sacrament of His love.

Let superficial and vain minds who so presumptuously take their stand on the progress of reason then see whither it led one of the deepest thinkers of this age.

In the face of such examples, how can the absurd prejudice be explained which maintains that Christian Faith is incompatible with the progress of reason and science?

We have seen, and still see at this moment, learned men, men of the highest intellect, the most illustrious savants of France, Germany, England, and America return to the Faith that never grows old, and, after having scrutinized all, tried all, proclaim that this Faith is the torch of science, the infallible guide of true progress. And are not those who have always kept the Faith of their baptism as strong in reasoning, as well informed in the progress of science, as the unbelievers among whom they live?

Science Is Not the Cause of Unbelief

Let men cease to justify their infidelity by seeking refuge in a pretended incompatibility between Catholic Faith and modern science. Such an excuse is unworthy of a sincere mind. The real causes of infidelity are not to be found in the progress of information. We will now endeavor to show what they are.

4

∞

Ignorance Is a Cause of Unbelief

Faith, as we have seen, is an act of the understanding, but an act prescribed by the will: a free act. The cause of unbelief may be in the understanding or in the will, or in both these faculties combined; that is to say, in the whole soul. We will begin, then, with the understanding: we will seek to discover how and in what degree the understanding acts upon the influence of the will; this will lead us to study the state of the will, and with that the state of the whole soul in infidels.

The first and most common cause of infidelity is ignorance of those truths that are the objects of faith. People know nothing of religion; they do not know what the Catholic Church — which keeps the Faith and prolongs the presence of Jesus Christ upon this earth — believes and teaches. In most cases, such ignorance is not wholly unprecedented. In the early ages of Christianity, many pagans, and among them many of the intellectual men of the time, reproached the disciples of the Incarnate Word with adoring the head of an ass!

Is it possible that, after eighteen hundred years of Christian civilization, in a society born and nourished in the lap of the Church, men are still to be met with who heap upon us reproaches equally senseless? We see beside us learned men; men who have conscientiously studied the religions of Greece, of ancient Rome, of Persia, India, Egypt, and who yet speak of the religion of Jesus Christ, of the religion that has civilized Europe and is the light of the world, as a man born blind might speak of colors. Surely this phenomenon, which we daily witness, is one of the most alarming mysteries of the moral world.

Religious ignorance, as a cause of infidelity, shows itself in various degrees. There is total ignorance, and there is partial ignorance. But the greater number of unbelievers are totally ignorant of the Christian religion and have scarcely a vague notion of religion in general. We have seen that at the time when the soul of Maine de Biran began seriously to turn toward God, he looked upon religion as a matter of feeling in which reason had no part. Before that time, the thoughts of the philosopher had never even glanced at the religious order; to him that order had no existence. As long as Augustin Thierry was an infidel, he studied history without any regard to religion — the only thing that can explain the history of the world. And when his eyes began to open, when he had a glimpse of the part assigned to religion, and thought he saw that religion could only be Christianity, he did not even then suspect that religious truth might be found in the Catholic Church. He knew nothing of the Church, or knew her only through the caricatures of her enemies. This man, who was so eager for knowledge, so curious in research, had never read with sincere attention a history of the Church, nor a complete and exact exposition of Catholic doctrine. How can men believe, when they know nothing of what they ought to believe?

M. Droz, a member of the French Academy, admits that he became an infidel, not in consequence of a serious examination of Christian truth, but without any examination, and because he was ill-informed with regard to the principles and doctrines of the Christian religion, ignorantly and unreservedly accepting all the opinions of infidelity. This was an unhappy age, in which many marvelously gifted youths became, in some sort, the necessary prey of irreligion as soon as they entered the world—many, alas! receiving their first lessons of infidelity at the domestic hearth.

Droz had received a Christian education; he had gone through his humanities and course of philosophy in a college where the doctrines and practices of Christianity were held in honor. Still he was almost wholly ignorant of religion, and the first assaults of infidelity destroyed his belief. He did not, however, sink to the depth of moral and religious degradation as so many others had done; his noble mind, while it rejected Christian revelation, preserved its belief in God, in the immortality of the soul, and in the moral law; he was one of the most upright and accomplished types of spiritualistic rationalism.

Let us listen to his confession; it will teach us how it happened that so many young men, at the beginning of the last century, became infidels, and how it happens, doubtless, that so many become infidels at this day:

> I was almost always inattentive to religious instruction, and was far from having given those solid foundations to my belief which the times in which we were living required. The philosophy of the eighteenth century was predominant. Deists, in order to exercise influence, had no need either of profound learning or close logic; irreligion was the fashion; infidelity and indifference seemed to be in the air we breathed. Whilst I was occupying myself with literature and prudently descending from poetry to

prose, I constantly heard so many voices repeat with full conviction, "The cause of Christianity has been judged and is lost forever," that I never doubted that I must start from this opinion as from a certain fact, when I would treat of religion with the enlightened men of the time. Thus did the youth of that time decide.

God might have punished me for my infidelity more severely than he has done; he might have suffered me to fall into the degradation of the sophists, who seek in their pitiful pride to maintain that God does not exist, that man acts under the dominion of fate, and that morality is but a fable invented by ingenious men to dupe the weak and foolish. I was spared this excess of degradation; God, whose goodness surpasses our sins; God, to whom I owe so many acts of thanksgiving; God has never wholly abandoned me.

Is it credible that this upright rationalist who was absorbed in the study of moral philosophy, and who read assiduously the essays of Montaigne, the *Tusculan Disputations* and *De Officiis* of Cicero, the *Dream of Scipio*, *Plutarch*, that he should never have dreamt of reading the Gospel, nor any of the great Christian moralists who have drawn freely from that incomparable source? In his eyes Christianity was irrevocably condemned, and all Christian literature was suppressed by the same blow. In this way did he understand and apply free examination.

I cannot forbear quoting one more page from the instructive *Aveux* of this once infidel moralist:

I did not lose time in seeking for arguments against Christianity; what was the use of doing so? Others had taken this trouble, and, as far as I was concerned, the question was settled. In all my projects, that which occupied me most was the desire to succeed in self-improvement. In spite of my love of literature and philosophy, far from paying a fanatical homage to Voltaire, the patriarch of irreligion, I was disgusted by his cynicism—I was grieved to behold an illustrious poet disgrace his genius by a parody of the history of the angelic heroine of France.... The so-called *Philosophy of History* excited still more painful feelings. In this libel against humanity, man is represented as a mass of vice, which renders him at once hateful and contemptible: what can be done with such a being? I loved liberty; I demanded it for all nations capable of understanding it; and when I saw the enthusiastic admirers of Voltaire proclaim themselves the champions of public liberty, the incoherency of their ideas confounded me. If man is made up of the tiger and the monkey, why should we speak of giving him liberty? On the contrary, bring a muzzle and chains; defend the world from the crimes of such a monster.[29]

We perceive that Droz, although an infidel, was not a follower of Voltaire. He was not a fanatic in his irreligion; he was an upright, moderate rationalist, striving to judge of men and things by the light of calm, serene reason. But he knew very little of the Christian religion, and unwittingly condemned it on the word of those disciples of Voltaire whom he held in such slight estimation. Question those learned and distinguished men who in our own days have passed from rationalism or Protestantism to

---

[29] François-Xavier-Joseph Droz, *Aveux d'un Philosophe Chrétien*, 17–18.

the Catholic Faith, ask them why they rejected, and sometimes with supreme contempt, the teaching of the Church? Most of them will answer that they were ill-informed in regard to that teaching; many, that they were wholly ignorant of it.

If such was the religious ignorance of unbelievers as earnest as Maine de Biran, Augustin Thierry, and Droz, what must we think of the ordinary run of infidels? It is a fact, of which the infidel press alone gives mournful evidence, that the generality of them do not even suspect what the Catholic religion may be. Ignorance in religious matters is truly a phenomenon.

Still a certain number of men are to be met with among infidels who are not ignorant of Catholic belief so far as this. They have some notion of the Christian revelation and of the doctrines it contains; they even find things in the life and teaching of the Church that command their admiration, but, seen under a false light, one point or other of the Catholic Creed or Catholic discipline stops them, and they remain in their unbelief.

Some minds reject the Christian Faith because the mystery of the Trinity or of Original Sin shocks their reason. Ask them how they understand the doctrine of the Church on these two dogmas that in our own opinion shed so valuable a light over history and philosophy, and you will at once perceive that they attach to these great mysteries a sense that is really repugnant to reason and that has nothing in common with the Catholic sense; men create phantoms for themselves and then shrink from them in horror.

How many infidels impute to the Church on the subject of Original Sin not only what she does not teach, but what she has formally condemned! Then they draw consequences from this travesty of the Catholic dogma that are really monstrous and that, if they were legitimately deduced from it, would, I admit, suffice to refute it in the eyes of all reasonable beings.

What just and generous soul, they exclaim, would not shudder at that necessary consequence of the dogma of original sin that infants who die unbaptized are punished eternally in hell like the greatest criminals? Were such a consequence well founded, I confess that I should be deeply disturbed by it. But in what general council, in what papal bull, in what scriptural or traditional source, in the writings of what authorized theologian, have they seen that such is the bearing of the Catholic dogma?

We most emphatically deny that the Church anywhere teaches that children who die with the sole taint of original sin are punished in the same way as men who have been guilty of grave personal sin and who quit this life in impenitence; the Church does not even teach that such children are positively unhappy.

There is a simple and supremely reasonable Catholic maxim, which is a kind of bugbear to many minds that in other respects seem to be well enough disposed toward the Church; it is the maxim *No salvation outside of the Church.*

But I repeat that this is but a necessary application of the most evident principles of reason, as soon as men admit that there is a religion revealed by God; nevertheless, we frequently see learned men who reject Catholicism, alleging this maxim as their excuse—they discover in it what no Catholic theologian has ever seen, the wholesale and blind condemnation of all who do not belong to the external communion of the Church. Were such the meaning of this dogma, I do not hesitate to declare that it would be as absurd as it is odious; but, thank God, it bears no such interpretation.

Sometimes it is a simple point of Catholic discipline that disturbs and arrests certain minds. They only half understand it — they only know it according to the estimation of persons who are hostile, or at least strangers, to the Church; but there they stop and gravely declare that, although Catholicism may have good points, it cannot be accepted as a whole.

How terrible a thing is prejudice! We Catholics are often reproached with obeying prejudices. I admit that in some respects we do obey prejudices, but as a celebrated controversialist of the seventeenth century[30] has remarked, there are reasonable prejudices and prejudices that are extremely unreasonable. Ask those who were formerly unbelievers but whose firm and generous faith now rejoices the Church of God whether they were not slaves of most blind prejudice, when, like you, they rejected the Catholic Faith? You will see what their answer will be. Why, then, do not you, who love truth and admire Christianity, if certain difficulties present themselves, ask an explanation from the teachers of that great religion which, for eighteen hundred years, has been the consolation and glory of the greatest geniuses of whom the world can boast?

Why do you not imitate the noble and generous mind of whom I spoke just now? Why not go as he did and confide your doubts, your hesitations, your difficulties, to one of your brethren whose charge it is to explain the teaching of this religion? What is there opposed to your dignity in such a course?

Listen to the confessions of Droz, deploring the fault he committed in seeking to escape from his ignorance and his doubts without having consulted anyone:

When I wished to begin the examination of Christianity, I had been so much accustomed to rely on my own light

[30] Paul Pellisson-Fontanier.

and guidance, that in my presumptuous ignorance I sought counsel of none to direct my researches. It is easy to see the utility of religion: its benefits are before our eyes; but instruction is necessary for the consideration of religion in itself, and to bring its truths home to ourselves. It was indispensable that a man who had been enlightened by its study should supply the light of which I was devoid. I knew a priest held in universal veneration; in my eagerness to escape from doubt I decided that I would see him the very next morning.... I opened my heart to him; I revealed to him my thoughts, my agitation, my desires, in all sincerity. I finished by saying to him: I owe to the proofs afforded by my feelings the desire that religion should be true. Finish by conveying to my understanding the entire conviction which my heart craves. But if, instead of seeking to convince my reason, you command me to believe — if I must sacrifice the noblest gift I have received from Heaven I have nothing more to ask you, we cannot understand one another.[31]

Thanks to the instructions of the priest, this suspicious rationalist soon learned that the Christian Faith does not sacrifice reason but takes it for granted, purifies, strengthens, extends, and elevates it; he understood that Faith demands but one sacrifice, the sacrifice of pride, which he confounded with reason.

[31] Droz, *Aveux d'un Philosophe Chrétien*, 65–66.

5

∽

Causes of Religion Indifference

It is a widespread opinion these days that error is not culpable and that no one is responsible for the religious ignorance in which he lives. This opinion is supremely absurd and shows too plainly the general decline of reason. Were it true, we should be obliged to declare that man is not a free agent, and that the truth has no claim upon his understanding. Our understanding, considered in itself, and apart from the will, is undoubtedly not free, but by its nature it is under the command of the will; it is placed under the direction of the will and participates in its freedom. Let it never be forgotten that the will is the central power and ruler of the soul, that from the will the whole soul must receive its impulse and direction, that it is made to rule and direct the movements of the understanding as well as the movements of the feelings and affections: everything must depend upon the will, and the will is responsible for everything. Therefore—it cannot be too often repeated—it is the will that really makes the man. Let no one say that all conditions of the understanding, all ignorance in matters of religion, are things indifferent in themselves; on the contrary, our intellectual state depends in a very great measure upon our will, and the ignorance of which we are speaking may be voluntary, and consequently culpable. Man is bound to know the truth, to adhere to it, to submit to it; whoever wills not seriously and sincerely to make use of the means at his disposal to arrive at the truth fails in his duty, and deserves punishment for his ignorance and his errors.

All ignorance of the religion revealed by God is assuredly not culpable. There are many souls to whom it is morally impossible to recognize the truth of the Church's teaching, either by reason of the condition in which they are living, or the atmosphere of prejudice that enveloped their early education, or of other circumstances absolutely independent of their will. God will not condemn these souls for that of which they are ignorant. Pius IX wrote as follows to the bishops of Italy:

> We know and you know that they who are unavoidably ignorant of our most Holy Religion, and who, carefully observing the natural law and the precepts engraved by God in the hearts of all men, and willing to obey God, lead an honest, upright life, may, with the help of Divine light and grace, acquire eternal life; for God, who perfectly sees, searches, and knows the minds, souls, thoughts, and actions of all men, in his sovereign goodness and clemency, permits not that he who is not guilty of a voluntary fault should suffer eternal punishment.[32]

It is a question of sincerity, of which God is the judge.

But religious ignorance frequently depends on moral causes that must be studied, and this study will afford us occasion to penetrate more profoundly into the mystery of unbelief. Infidelity

---

[32] Pius IX, Encyclical letter *Quanto Conficiamur Moerore* (On Promotion of False Doctrines), August 10, 1863.

is a complex fact in which all the powers of the soul have a share. As we proceed, we shall be more and more convinced of this fundamental truth. We will begin by pointing out a general condition of the soul very common among unbelievers; next, we will show by what means many souls descend all the steps of unbelief until they lose themselves in materialism, or perish in the helplessness of skepticism or the aberrations of pantheism. We will then return to the consideration of the moral obstacles that the Christian Faith meets with in the souls of the better class of infidels — of those who admit the fundamental dogmas of natural religion.

Levity of mind, moral dissipation, a culpable indifference to religion: these are the ordinary sources of religious ignorance and among the most common causes of infidelity. What are the greater number of men who do not believe doing? What is the usual condition of their souls? The apostle St. John wrote to the first disciples of the gospel: "Love not the world, nor the things that are in the world.... All that is in the world is the concupiscence of the flesh, and the concupiscence of the eyes, and the pride of life."[33] The world, in the language of Scripture, denotes men "who prefer visible and transitory things to those that are invisible and eternal."[34] This world ever exists, and although the triple concupiscence that the apostle points out has in some respects diminished during the long reign of the Christian Faith, it still displays itself in the world and still brings forth therein the fruit of death. Are not the pleasures of sense, riches, honors, the sole object of desire and pursuit to the ordinary run of unbelievers?

[33] 1 John 2:15–16.
[34] Jacques Bénigne Bossuet, *Traité de la Concupiscence*, chap. 1.

Unbelief

Material interests, considered under their diverse forms, absorb them wholly. They occupy themselves only with perishable goods; this present life is everything to them. Probably they do not deny that there is a future life, but they think nothing about it; it is an item that does not enter into their calculations. To succeed in the world, to satiate themselves with riches, with pleasure, and, if possible, with glory, or at any rate with honors, is their sole care. Some give themselves up with a kind of frenzy to sensual enjoyment; a great number exercise a kind of half restraint upon themselves and at least respect decency, although their view extends not beyond the narrow horizon of this earth. With such dispositions, men are capable of sinking to the lowest depths of degradation, but they will not raise themselves to the heights of the moral order to seek the light of truth. Such men as these do not even dream of studying religion.

Pascal said of the few infidels of his time:

> We know well enough how men of this kind act. They think they have made great efforts at self-instruction if they have spent a few hours in reading the Scriptures and have questioned some ecclesiastic on the truths of Faith. Afterward they boast of having made a fruitless search in books and among men. But, in truth, I cannot refrain from telling them, as I have often done, that such negligence is intolerable. The trifling interests of some stranger are not in question here; the stake is ourselves and our all.
>
> This negligence in a manner which concerns themselves, their eternity, their all, irritates more than it moves me; it astonishes me, it alarms me. To me it is monstrous.[35]

---

[35] Blaise Pascal, *Pensées* 2, 2.

What would the religious and austere solitary of Port Royal say if he lived in our days? It is no longer a question with the multitude of unbelievers of employing some hours in reading the Scriptures and questioning some ecclesiastic on the truths of Faith. They read nothing; they question no one; they take no thought of religion. There is a levity and indifference about them inexplicable in reasonable beings. "There must be strange disorder in a man's nature who can live in such a state, still more when he can pride himself on it."[36]

And yet the greater number do really pride themselves on it. They despise us who believe; they denounce us as the enemies of reason, as men whose understandings are enslaved; whilst they look upon themselves as reason personified, claim for themselves alone liberty of thought, and proudly call themselves freethinkers. From the time of La Bruyère infidels have called themselves *esprits forts*; this title called forth from the immortal author of *Les Caractères* the following reflection:

Do our *esprits forts* know that they are called thus in irony? God forbid that I should wish to offend anyone, but I cannot help seeing the most bitter irony in the name of freethinkers as given to infidels. It is a fact that the generality of them think neither freely nor servilely; they do not think at all.

Permit me to say frankly that there are infinitely more free-livers than freethinkers among the enemies of the Christian Faith. If some few (and they are the exception) really think, I know of nothing less free than their thoughts; they are the slaves of the blindest and most

---

[36] Pascal.

absurd prejudices; they accept, with a truly blind faith, all the judgments which condemn Christianity.

An infidel examining the bases of the Christian Religion, sincerely, without prepossession, with conscientious freedom, is the rarest thing in the world. When a man has done that, he is very near renouncing infidelity and embracing the Faith.

But, I repeat, this multitude of worshippers of free examination, and these so-called freethinkers examine nothing and never think for themselves. They repeat lofty maxims, write pompous formulae, for the most part like parrots, and without attaching any meaning to them; this is the power and freedom of their thought in the domain of morals and religion.

They affirm with imperturbable assurance that they are for the independence of reason, for the emancipation of the human mind, for progress, for the liberty of nations; according to them, the Catholic Faith is the antithesis of these beautiful and noble things. But do not ask them what they mean by the independence of reason, the emancipation of the human mind, and other articles of the rationalist program; they are words which they repeat by heart and without having ever examined their true meaning.

Above all, do not ask them in what the Catholic Faith, which is professed by the most independent, purest, and most eminent men of our days, as it was in the days of St. Augustine — do not ask them in what that Faith opposes the freedom of reason and shackles social progress. They have never thought of it; they will give you no other answer than the eternal sing-song of accusations a hundred times refuted, and formulas as new as the formula which comprises all the religious science of the disciples of Mohammed: God is God, and Mohammed is his prophet.[37]

We will close this chapter with one general observation. The meaning of words must be restored. What man in his senses would say that moral freedom consists in exemption from the rule of virtue? How, then, can men place intellectual liberty in exemption from the rule of truth? For pity's sake, do not confound liberty with libertinism. There is a libertinism of thought as well as a libertinism of morals. To live regardless of the law of virtue is moral libertinism; to think and speak without regard for the law of truth is intellectual libertinism.

We will now see where either one or the other may lead.

[37] Jean de la Bruyère, *Caractères*, chap. 16.

6

∽

Materialism

The ordinary result of the intellectual levity and moral dissipation that we have just described is to materialize the soul and to lead it to believe only in sensible realities. There is a twofold materialism—a *dogmatic materialism*, which denies positively the existence of the soul and of God, and a *practical materialism*, which denies neither the one nor the other expressly, but neglects and forgets them both. The moral condition, of which we have just spoken, cannot be distinguished from this practical materialism. We will now speak of dogmatic materialism, properly so called.

This materialism, which for a short time was ignominiously driven from the schools of infidel philosophy, has reappeared in the last few years and has again acquired considerable influence. It is daily gaining ground in the domain of natural science, and many cultivated minds are ranging themselves under its banner. Now, materialism is radical infidelity—it is the denial of the very foundation on which all religion rests, and on which the Christian Faith in particular must take its stand.

How can a soul come to ignore and deny its own existence? How can it sink to this intellectual and moral degradation? The key to this mystery must be sought for in human liberty, which is the principle of all degradation and all elevation. We are free and imperfect beings; we may refuse our adherence to truths of the moral order, and our soul may so far blind itself not all at once, but by dint of a thousand weak and base acts that at length it will come to ignore God and no longer be able to discern itself. Men reach this point by two roads: by libertinism of life, and also, while preserving a comparatively virtuous exterior, by that religious indifference that enervates the best part of the soul and ends by extinguishing its life.

Our soul has a direct and immediate view of itself; it has a perception of itself, the manifestations of its life, its understanding, its sensibility, and its will; it perceives God and the moral order by evidence that seems irresistible. How then is materialism possible? It arises from the moral condition of the soul; it comes from this: that the state of our understanding depends in great measure on the state of our will and affections. All our faculties are mutually affected and exercise an incessant action upon one another. Nothing is easier than to refute a materialist, but it is not so easy to cure him. This cure is possible only by means of a moral treatment that is occasionally very painful.

There are souls so buried in matter, so materialized, that the realities of the moral world have no longer any meaning to them but appear to them the most inexplicable chimera. The most sublime religious symbols reveal absolutely nothing to them: in the most touching ceremonies of religion they behold merely external things, having no moral significance.

A Russian of great distinction who was converted a few years ago to the Catholic Faith attests this of himself: M. Schouvaloff had in his youth lost all religious belief. Not only did he no longer believe the gospel, but he no longer recognized the existence either of God or of his own soul. Teachers of philosophy had confirmed him in his denial of the truth. He passed several years in this state. In the history of his life he says:

> As I finish the account of this first part of my spiritual existence, I ask myself how it happened that neither my heart nor my mind was ever touched, when, during my sojourn in Italy, and particularly in Rome, I happened to be present at religious ceremonies.
>
> I cannot comprehend my indifference in this respect, nor how it happened that no serious idea ever came to me — to me who believed myself to be a thoughtful man at the sight of things that had been objects of veneration for so many centuries, and that to men belonging to all classes of society, to every degree of intelligence.
>
> It is true that I never entered a church except out of curiosity or from some other frivolous motive, but still I went into the churches; I was present at glorious and beautiful ceremonies; my eyes were sometimes arrested by ancient sculptures or magnificent pictures, the figures of which, seen through clouds of incense, appeared animated with life; everywhere was to be seen the image of the Holy Mother, surrounded with innumerable *ex voto*, tokens of hope, of sorrow, of gratitude, and of love; the most profound feelings of the heart had left their traces on her altars.
>
> Moreover, I heard words, sublime in their simplicity, mingling with the music of angels; the air of the basilicas appeared to me to be impregnated with the sentiment of Faith; here, a whole people listened motionless to the voice of the preacher; there, the faithful were confessing

their sins; others, with silent devout recollection, were receiving the Divine Body; prostrate priests adored the Sacred Host; an old man, the Father of Christians, washed the feet of a few poor men, or gave his benediction to the city and to the world.... And in presence of these grand spectacles not a thought, not a question! I beheld them with the indifference of idiocy.... One sense was wanting — the spiritual sense, the divine sense! My body was present, but my soul was elsewhere.... It slept.

This is truly the condition of a materialized soul; in it the moral sense is, as it were, extinct. Still, the root of this sense is alive but is stifled by foreign elements. To restore its vigor, these elements must be removed, and the soul must be replaced in its true position. This is the object of the moral treatment of which I was speaking just now.

Plato was perfectly well acquainted with materialized minds; they abounded in pagan society.

He has depicted them in several passages of his *Dialogues*, but particularly in the celebrated allegory of the cave. The great moralist compares this visible world to a subterranean cave, in which men who have been in chains since infancy behold the shadows of objects through an opening and by the pale glimmer of a fire; the captives imagine that these shadows are the only realities.

Now see [continues Plato] what must naturally happen if they be delivered from their chains and cured of their error. Let one of these captives be unbound: let him be compelled to stand up at once, to turn his head, to walk, and to turn to the light. He will do all this with infinite trouble; the light will hurt his eyes, and dazzle him so as to prevent his discerning the objects whose shadows he formerly beheld. What think you might he reply to him who should tell him that up to this time he had seen only phantoms, but that now he has more real objects, objects more approaching to the truth, before his eyes? Suppose he were now pulled out of the cavern and dragged by a rude, steep path to the light of the sun, what a punishment would it be to him! How great would be his fury! And when he should have reached the light of day, would not his eyes be dazzled by the brightness? Could he see anything of the crowd of objects which we call real beings? At first he would not be able to do so. Doubtless time would be necessary to accustom him to it.

But when he had become accustomed to the sight of objects, and to the contemplation of the sun which gives them light, if he happened to call to mind his first dwelling, the companions of his slavery, and the idea which they had there of wisdom, would he not rejoice in his own change? Would he not compassionate their misfortune? Most assuredly he would. Do you think he would still be jealous of the honors, praise and rewards given to him who was most prompt in seizing the shadows as they passed, or who called to mind most accurately which shadows went before, which followed, which went together, and thus was the most skillful in guessing the time of their appearance; or that he envied their condition who were most powerful and most honored in that prison? Would he not prefer passing his life, as is related of Achilles by Homer, in the service of a poor laborer, and suffer everything rather than resume his former condition, with its illusions? I doubt not that he would be ready to suffer everything rather than again live in that manner.... Well, my dear Glaucus, that is the precise image of our human state. The subterranean cave is this visible world; the fire by which it is lighted is the light of the sun; the captive who soars to a higher region and who contemplates it is the soul raising itself to the sphere of intelligence.[38]

The materialized soul delights in this kingdom of shadows, which it takes for the only realities and is irritated by any proposal to quit this world of phantoms. Only at the price of a generous effort can it be snatched from them. The fulfillment of a moral condition must be the first step; the soul must purify itself and disengage itself as much as possible from the mass of gross images that defile its sight and hinder it from contemplating the true light. In the *Phaedo*, Socrates, discoursing on his approaching death, and seeking to console his friends, defines the purification of the soul to be a kind of anticipated death:

Does not the purification of the soul consist in separating it as much as possible from the body; in accustoming it to be shut up in itself, to be recollected in itself, and to live as much as possible ... alone and in itself, disengaged from the shackles of the body?... Without the least doubt this is so.[39]

"Now, what is death," adds Socrates, "if not the complete separation of the soul and body? The philosopher who seeks to purify his soul exercises himself in dying, and philosophy is an apprenticeship of death."[40] The illustrious sage of Athens had

[38] Plato, *Republic* 7.
[39] *Phaedo* 67.
[40] *Phaedo*. Cicero and the Neoplatonists reproduced this maxim.

but a glimpse of this sublime thought, which was to be fully comprehended and realized free from all admixture of error by Christianity alone.

Plato recognizes three distinct principles in the soul of man: the superior or rational part of the soul is the seat of the understanding; the inferior part is the seat of sensation and material pleasures; the middle part is the seat of passions somewhat more elevated, such as anger, pride, and ambition.[41] For the man who seeks truth he teaches the necessity of subjecting the lower and middle parts of the soul to the superior, so that, free from all shackles, it may more easily turn to the contemplation of that which is. Says Socrates:

> Have you not yet remarked how far the sagacity of those men reaches to whom is given the name of clever rogues? With what penetration does their little soul seize on the things to which it is turned. Its sight is by no means weak, but as they constrain it to serve their malice, the more penetrating it is, the more hurtful it is. This is most true. But take these same souls from childhood, cut and pare away all that the passions of lust have deposited therein, loosen them from the heavy masses attached to the pleasures of the table and similar luxuries, take away the weight which depresses the glance of the soul to inferior things; then if the same glance in the same souls, freed from these obstacles, is turned toward the things that are true, it will behold them with the same penetration with which it now beholds these things to which it is turned.[42]

---

[41] *Republic* 9.
[42] *Republic* 7.

Unbelief

The faculty of knowing God and moral truths is implanted in man; but it is weakened, paralyzed in its movements, turned away from its object, by the weight of sensual passions or by material prepossessions. To restore to this noble faculty, its power of soaring on high, and to enable it to turn toward its true object, it is necessary to combat these passions and to triumph over these strange prepossessions.

Man must be purified by mortification. Those who do not purify themselves spend their lives in miserably passing from the lower to the middle region of the soul, and in falling back again from the middle to the lower region, without ever raising themselves to that where God manifests Himself.

Men who know neither wisdom nor virtue, who are always taken up with festivities and other sensual pleasures, necessarily sink to the lowest region; thence they raise themselves to the middle region, and pass their lives in wandering between the two. But to traverse these two regions in order to look upon that which is really on high, and to raise themselves to it, this is what they never do. Therefore, they have never been filled with the possession of that which truly is, nor have they ever tasted a pure and solid joy. Bent down toward the earth, like animals whose eyes are ever fixed upon their food, they give themselves up brutally to good cheer and love; they dispute among themselves for the enjoyment of these pleasures, turn their arms against one another, and end in mutual slaughter.... You have just sketched the condition of the greater number of men. Does not the same thing necessarily occur with regard to that part of the soul where courage resides when ambition, seconded by jealousy, the spirit of strife by violence, and a savage disposition by anger, drive man without reflection or discernment to pursue a false plenitude of honor and victory, and afterward to the satisfying of his resentment? The same thing must necessarily happen.[43]

How many men run after this false plenitude of honor and victory, and, willing captives, know not how to surmount the narrow frontiers of that cavern that can offer them only shadows!

It is assuredly not absolutely necessary that the soul should be freed from the yoke of passions and interests before it can recognize God and the moral order, but it has need of a certain degree of purification to raise itself to that superior world and to attach itself thereto by a firm adherence of the understanding. When a soul has attained this moral condition, it must, by an act of the will, unfold its divine faculty and direct it on the object for which the soul is made. This is a movement that purification renders easy and that completes the education of the soul. What is the use of the organ of sight if men do not make use of it, or if it is ill-directed? Says Plato once more:

> In the evolution which is given to the soul, the whole art consists in turning it in the easiest and most beneficial manner. The question is not to bestow on it the faculty of sight — it has that already; but its organ is in a bad direction, it does not look in the right direction.... The faculty of knowledge ... never loses its power, only it becomes useful and advantageous, or useless and hurtful according to the direction which is given to it.[44]

---

[43] *Republic* 9.
[44] *Republic* 7.

Unbelief

This is the real supreme importance of the part that the will bears in knowledge. Would that those poor souls who deny God and ignore themselves would seriously reflect upon it!

7

∞

Causes of Skepticism

How few souls are there, in these days, who preserve their equilibrium and their uprightness, affirming what ought to be affirmed, denying what ought to be denied, abstaining from judging where it is right so to abstain! Aristotle has defined virtue to be the middle between the two vices of too much and too little.[45] I do not accept this definition in its full extent, but it is frequently no less applicable in the intellectual than in the moral life. Sometimes men foolishly seek to raise themselves, alone and without support, above human nature; sometimes they sink below that same nature by falling miserably into materialism or skepticism. How many minds are in perpetual oscillation between these two extremes, slipping now on one side, now on the other, without power to fix themselves in the just medium that reason prescribes!

Skepticism often depends on a moral condition similar to that which engenders and nourishes materialism; occasionally, however, it arises from other causes. I am now speaking of moral universal skepticism, of that state of mind that denies nothing positively but at the same time does not affirm any truth of the

[45] Aristotle, *Nicomachean Ethics* 2, 6.

moral order, whether natural or supernatural; in which a man doubts the existence of God, of his own soul, of all religious principles. With some men, universal doubt is the result of a false system of philosophy carried out to its extreme point, but this is an exception that we need not specially notice. Even in minds that give themselves up to philosophical studies and are sincerely prepossessed in favor of the truth, skepticism is rarely the logical product of a false method. It almost always depends on other causes; it springs for the most part from a monstrous and bitter deception. It is this deception that directly engenders intellectual despair; but in this it is assisted by moral dispositions that indicate an unhealthy condition of the soul. Skepticism is a weakness of the will and of the understanding. It is the younger son of pride, if I may so speak.

Pride begins with a ridiculous self-sufficiency and ends in despair. This is, in one word, the history of many skeptics of lofty and earnest intelligence. In this way, as we have already seen, St. Augustine fell into skepticism. Disdaining the Christian Faith, he at first imagined that he should be able to discover everything by reason alone. When deceived in this presumptuous confidence, that noble genius recoiled upon itself, and took up the belief that the human understanding is powerless to attain a certain knowledge of truth. How many infidels, in our own days and under our own eyes, have gone through this same experience! Their reason, jealous of a false independence, sought to walk alone to the conquest of all truths, and rejected with disdain the support of Divine Authority. And in what did this course generally end? For the most part, in miserable discouragement and bitter despair.

I will content myself with recalling the example of Théodore Jouffroy, one of the most eminent philosophers of the school of

French rationalists. Jouffroy had received a Catholic education, but his belief was weak and unenlightened and vanished at the first breath of rationalistic teaching. His young and ardent mind, seduced by the false promises of infidel philosophy, was persuaded that it was about to find, in that philosophy, the clear and definite solution of all problems. Wrote the disappointed philosopher at a later period:

> My mind was persuaded that on entering upon the study of philosophy it was about to encounter a regular science, which, after having pointed out its end and the process by which to attain it, would conduct me by a sure and well-defined road to the certain knowledge of those things which are of surpassing interest to man. In one word, my understanding, excited by its necessities and enlarged by the teaching of Christianity, had ascribed to philosophy the grand object, the vast framework, the sublime bearing of a religion.... Such had been my hope; and what did I find? The struggle which had awakened the slumbering echoes of the faculty, and which had turned the heads of all my fellow-students, had for its object — its sole object — the question of the origin of ideas. I could not recover from my astonishment that men should occupy themselves with the origin of ideas with as much ardor as if the whole of philosophy was contained in it,[46] *and yet leave on one side man, God, the world, and the relations which unite them to the enigma of the past and the mysteries*

---

[46] It must not be forgotten that in rationalism, philosophy takes the place of religion and ought consequently to fulfill the task of religion.

of the future, and to many other gigantic problems on which
they did not conceal their skepticism.

All philosophy seemed to be buried in a hole where
there was no air, and in which my soul, recently exiled
from Christianity, was stifled, yet the authority of the
teachers and the fervor of their disciples impressed
me, and I dared not show either my surprise or my
disappointment.[47]

Jouffroy soon became one of the most distinguished masters
of that philosophy that assumed itself to be the supreme personi-
fication of reason. His personal researches could not fill up the
void that the loss of faith had produced in his soul. All religious
certainty had disappeared from his mind. He became a skeptic:
God, man, the world, their mutual relations, all those grand
problems that every intelligent soul necessarily proposes to itself
remained obscure enigmas to him. Listen to the philosopher
telling, with the accent of despair, the impression that the sight
of the places where he had once had the happiness to live as a
Christian made upon his afflicted soul. He says:

I found myself once more under the roof where I had
passed my childhood, in the midst of those who had
brought me up so tenderly, in the presence of objects
which had struck my eyes, touched my heart, affected my
understanding, in the happy days of my early life.... All
was unchanged except myself.

The Church, where the holy mysteries were celebrated
with the same devotion; the fields, the woods, the foun-
tains which were still blessed in the springtime; the house

[47] Théodore Jouffroy, *Mélanges Philosophiques.*

where, on the appointed day, an altar of flowers and foliage was still erected; the Curé, who had instructed me in the Faith and who had grown old, was still there, still firm in his belief; all who surrounded me had the same heart, the same soul, the same hope in faith. I alone had lost it. *I alone lived without knowing how or why. I alone, so learned, knew nothing. I alone was empty, agitated, deprived of light, blind, and restless.*[48]

This is what rationalism had effected in an understanding naturally so powerful and enlightened.

These last words of Jouffroy, so profoundly mournful, remind me of the observation of another philosopher who was also for some time an infidel, but who returned at last to the Faith of his childhood. M. Droz says:

I was often astonished to see illustrious philosophers less enlightened on the most important subjects than humble Christians. Is it not shameful that sages should consume long watches in seeking what has been long ago found? Philosophers discuss the question as to what is man's destination upon earth; they plunge into subtleties, they exhaust themselves in declamations more or less eloquent, and in the meanwhile a good Christian woman would say to them: God has created us to love him and to worship him, and to make us one day participate in his felicity. Here we are in a place of probation where duties are imposed upon us; we may fulfil them or we may transgress them. After this short life, according as we shall have

[48] Work quoted by M. Guizot in his *Méditations et Études Morales*, preface.

obeyed or resisted the will of our Father, he will reward us because he is good, or he will punish us because he is just. If philosophers do not confine themselves to the development of these words in treating the same subject, they unteach us the truth.[49]

Jouffroy was unable to recover from his fall into skepticism. This proud philosopher concludes his works by charging philosophy with absolute impotence; he ends by declaring with bitter sadness that philosophy, which in his idea is the same thing as rationalism, raises and brings to light a multitude of questions, none of which it is able to resolve. What a lesson is this! Men begin by proclaiming the omnipotence of human reason and end by accusing it of utter weakness. This is surely the well-deserved chastisement of pride, which in its delirium refuses to accept the conditions that God has imposed upon our nature, and disdain, which fully rejects the hand that alone can save us. Neither so high nor so low is the teaching of good sense and the teaching of Catholic philosophy. Rationalism is neither reason nor philosophy; it is the moral enemy of both; it compromises them and destroys them by its exaggeration and its foibles.

The causes of skepticism are complex; it is not produced in the same way in all minds that are attacked by this terrible malady. In the case of most infidels, it is not the result of a serious search after truth, but of an ill-directed search; it is the fruit of levity, of dissipation, of indolence of the will, or of a false direction of the understanding.

Many Christians who are not familiar with psychological studies ask themselves if skepticism is really possible and are

---

[49] Drox, *Aveux d'un Philosophe Chrétien*, 32–33.

astonished that earnest men can fall into such error. I can understand this blessed ignorance of evil. The faculties in a Christian soul are in equilibrium; they are maintained in their vigor and in their normal state. Skepticism, which is the overthrow and ruin of our moral and intellectual nature, is an impossibility in such a condition. But let a man enter into himself and scrutinize his own thoughts, let him study attentively the history of those souls who are not settled in the truth by Faith, and he will soon be convinced that skepticism is unfortunately but too possible, and that it is easier to become the prey of this monster than people usually imagine.

Let it never be forgotten that man is as free in his adherence to truth as he is in his adherence to virtue; in both orders it is possible to fall away. Men may reject what is true as they may reject what is good; they may hesitate and vacillate in affirming what is true, as well as in practicing what is good.

All truths, even those that we call evident, and that in reality are so, present a dark side to human reason; man, according to the saying of Montaigne, sees the whole of nothing. Even in the purely natural order, every object of human thought presents two faces—two sides: one clear, luminous, evident; the other dark and cloudy. I see a man; I affirm his existence; I affirm that he is a being composed of two distinct substances, body and soul. This affirmation rests on evidence. But when I affirm the existence of the body, when I affirm the existence of the soul, do I know which is the precise object of this twofold affirmation? I know it in a certain degree. I know which are the proper characteristics of the body. I know which are the essential properties of the soul. I see clearly that they are two distinct substances. But if I am asked to state in clear and forcible terms in what the essence of the human body consists, what constitutes its life, what the action of the organs of the body is, and how it is produced; if I am asked to define with the utmost precision the essence of my own soul, and to explain the play of all its faculties, I confess that I have no answer to give. I could certainly give a few explanations and elucidations, but I should soon come to a point before which I should be obliged to pause, and a grain of sand stops me as much as man. What philosopher dares to flatter himself that he knows thoroughly, and in all their parts, those things whose reality he affirms? A mysterious obscurity hangs over all our knowledge. One of the leaders of French rationalism has said with great truth, "In science, as often as we make any advance, we find an abyss; only weak minds believe that they can explain all and understand all."[50]

If nature herself, bounded, limited, finite as she is, conceals depths that our minds cannot fathom, must not God, the Infinite Being, be full of obscurity to us? No truth can be more easily demonstrated than the existence of God. But what incomprehensible things are there in the nature of that God whose existence reason demonstrates! Jules Simon, judging in this respect of the pretensions to omniscience that many of his companions in rationalism set up, says:

> More humiliated by what is wanting to us than intoxicated by that which we are permitted to discover, the first word we shall pronounce when we speak of God is *incomprehensibility*.
>
> Human pride, and we must also say philosophical pride, revolts at this word. We are willing enough to admit that religion speaks of the incomprehensibility of God,

---

[50] Jules Simon, *La Religion Naturelle*, 45.

and everyone knows that the Catholic Religion proclaims a hidden God—an incomprehensible God; but it would seem that the very end of philosophy is to explain all mysteries, to render all ideas precise, to carry everywhere the light of reason, and to accustom the human mind to believe only what it can prove and understand. We might say that Bayle's proverb, *Understanding is the measure of belief,* is the very motto of philosophy. To believe without proof or to believe without understanding appears to human reason to be at most only two different modes of abdicating its claims....

These commonplaces cannot stand examination. In science, the question is not to attain what we wish, but to attain what we can. No doubt the essence of philosophy consists in believing nothing without proof; but when the existence of a being is once proved, are we to renounce our belief in that existence on the pretext that the nature of that being is incomprehensible to us?... These data are so simple and natural that when we reflect on them we know not how to explain the pretensions to omniscience which certain schools have set up.[51]

"If in nature herself," adds the philosopher,

that is to say, in what is necessarily limited and imperfect, we admit the existence of real mysteries unfathomable to human reason, by what mental aberration would we have the only perfect Being to be without abysses which our thoughts cannot penetrate?

[51] Ibid., 35–40.

Unbelief

My life is passed at the bottom of an abyss, in the midst of mysteries. I am surrounded by the unknown; I am myself ever unknown to my own mind (in the sense in which we spoke just now). In spite of all this I live in peace. I speak of science in pompous terms, and when I come to demonstrate the existence of God and am told that he is incomprehensible, I cry out and declare myself offended in my dignity as a human being and as a philosopher.

No one could express this better. In these passages the author of *La Religion Naturelle* does but declare a well-known truth—one that has been recalled and explained a hundred times by Christian philosophers, but it is a truth big with consequences and has always more or less affrighted rationalism.

This, then, is the condition of human reason. We meet with mystery even in the dogmas of natural religion—in things that seem the most familiar to us. What must we do in the presence of that obscurity that in all our knowledge mingles constantly with the light? Must I deny or abstain from affirming the existence of God because I can comprehend His nature only in part? It is undeniable that I can do so. The obscurity that accompanies light, and to which our intelligence is averse, makes this denial possible, and leaves me at liberty to give or refuse my consent to the known truth. All depends on the disposition of my will.

We know what skepticism is. It will not accept a light mingled with shadows; it rejects the light out of fear and hatred of darkness. A reasonable man will not act thus. He admits the obscurity, which is inseparable from all knowledge; he admits it, not for itself, but on the authority of the light. He knows that he is not intended to understand everything. We are intelligent beings, no doubt, but we are also finite beings, and consequently the comprehension with which we are endowed is finite.

Also, further, we are beings subject to trial; and this state of probation excludes the full light of day. We mistake the laws of our nature and of our actual condition if we deny the existence of God because His nature is incomprehensible to us. Such pride would be ridiculous were it not profoundly criminal.

Occasionally skepticism springs less from pride than from a false direction of the understanding. Some minds prefer to direct and arrest their attention to what is obscure, with regard not only to moral and religious truths but to historical facts and questions of natural science. They will not look at the light, or scarcely glance at it; they fix their eyes only on the shadows. Is it astonishing if they do not see, or if they hesitate and grope their way along like the blind? We know many such minds. Things that are the most evident, the most solidly demonstrated, appear doubtful to them, because they do not see arguments but pay attention to a thousand little difficulties in which their darkened reason perplexes itself and ends by losing its way completely. Why not look on the side where light is?

We have said already that levity, indifference, and apathy, generally helped and fed by the passions, are the most frequent causes of religious skepticism. Men do not love the truth; they do not desire it — they fear it and turn away from it as from an enemy. With such dispositions, without the special aid of God, how can they avoid becoming skeptics? But let them not deceive themselves; such a skepticism is highly criminal, and the truth, from which they now fly, will one day find them out to their cost.

One who had traversed all the phases of infidelity has said: "The greatest benefit of religion is to save us from doubt and uncertainty.... All is uncertain, fugitive and changeable in a mind

Unbelief

destitute of religious belief."[52] Change, instability, fluctuation, is a malady of the understanding as well as of the heart of man; faith cures us of this malady by fixing our mind upon truth and prohibiting doubt: those who do not believe are but too frequently its victims. Therefore, says an Italian philosopher,

the Catholic precept is wisest which forbids us to admit a doubt of the known truth even for a single instant. The weakness and instability of the human mind are such, and so great, that, however strong and solid our persuasion of the truth of any article of faith may be, there is not one with regard to which difficulties may not sometimes arise capable of making a momentary impression on the mind; if men entertain this impression, doubting of the truth which they possess, they will by degrees acquire a habit of skepticism which will soon leave no belief intact. But if, on the contrary, they courageously resist these as-saults—if they despise these involuntary clouds of the mind—by degrees the darkness will disperse, calm will return, they will be able to smile at their doubts instead of thinking them formidable, and will wonder that they ever looked on them in a serious light. Sophistry sometimes assumes a specious and seductive aspect in the eyes of the understanding, as the passions do in the eyes of the heart; but if men are strong and do not yield to appearances, it will soon vanish away.[53]

[52] Maine de Biran, *Journal Intime*, 333.
[53] Vincenzo Gioberti.

8

∞

Sophistry and Its Victims

The understanding may become corrupted as well as the heart, but this is a case of less frequent occurrence. We have, however, signal examples of this corruption of the understanding in our day. This corruption is at once the root and the fruit of sophistry. I have no desire to go over the subject of modern sophistry, which my friend Father Gratry has treated in so masterly a manner; but after having, in the words of this uncompromising religious writer, pointed out the evil, I will seek to indicate the remedy.

> The sophists of the eighteenth century attacked the Faith in the name of reason; those of the nineteenth now attack reason itself. The sophists follow in the intellectual order the course which, according to Tacitus, they follow in the political order: they attack reasonable life in the same manner as they attack social life. "They first attack power," says Tacitus, "in the name of liberty, and when power has been overcome they attack liberty itself."[54] We see the same thing before our eyes in the intellectual

---

[54] Cornelius Tacitus, *Annals* 16, 22.

order. At first they attacked the power and authority of Faith in the name of reason; now they attack the free and manifest light of reason. At first they rejected the Eternal Word illuminating the assembly of Christians with his revelations; now they attack the Word, who, as the eternal light of reason, enlightens every man coming into this world.... Such is the progress of intellectual decay.

It is certain that *the absurd*, set forth daringly, openly, and without evasion, has sometimes a strange power. It has the fascination of a precipice. I know many instances of it. When a mind has once had the weakness to hesitate for an instant in presence of the visibly absurd, that mind is lost. As there is nothing more to expect, in the order of thought, from a mind which demands the demonstration of evidence, so there is nothing more to hope for from a mind which demands the refutation of the absurd, which is itself the evidence of error. Beyond evidence there is nothing to demonstrate; beyond the absurd there is nothing to refute.

There philosophy stops. Then the mind, deprived of the support of evidence, and of the beacon-light of the absurd, quits the limits of reason, and abandons philosophy for sophistry.... And what is sophistry? It is the process of a reason overthrown, which asks the demonstration of evidence, and which in the meanwhile denies evidence; which demands the refutation of the absurd, and which in the meanwhile affirms the absurd.[55]

---

[55] Auguste Joseph Alphonse Gratry, *Une Étude sur la Sophistique Contemporaine*, 124–126.

Sophistry and Its Victims

It is not that, as in materialism and skepticism, the soul is simply hebetated or enfeebled; sophistry is the perversion and utter overthrow of the mind. All is reversed; the fundamental principles of reason are overthrown, and the understanding, as it were, uprooted, floats in darkness and feeds upon contradictions. Hegel is the great master of sophistry, as we stated before, on the subject of pantheism. Hegel has founded in the midst of our Christian Europe a sophistry infinitely more dangerous than that of Gorgias and the other Greek sophists whom Socrates and Plato opposed. He has ruined innumerable minds. Father Gratry says once more:

> When a mind under the influence of Hegelianism, which is the most daring and at the same time the most radical form of sophistry, has once given way, and destroyed the two extreme limits of reason, which are evidence and the absurd, that mind — whatever may be its riches, its distinction, its natural qualities — that mind is lost. You can no longer reckon upon its judgment. To it assertion and contradiction are alike. It seeks contradiction methodically. Philosophy is now out of the question: the mind is occupied only with that sterile movement of thought of, for, or against, which Plato in the Sophist calls in derision "enantiopoiology."[56]

This sophistry, whose effects are before our eyes, springs directly from pantheism; it is the necessary application of the only logic that that cloudy system has to show that lays down as a thesis the identity of God and the world, of the necessary and the contingent, of the absolute and the relative, and thus terminates

---

[56] Ibid., 126–127.

fatally in the confusion of truth and falsehood, good and evil, being and non-existence. Pantheism is the doctrine of universal identity or general confusion. In this pretended philosophy, light and darkness, day and night, are but one and the same thing. Hegel affirms this in express terms in his logic. It is the direct negation of reason, of what humanity in all times has always called reason.

For some years past pantheism has in a remarkable degree lost its prestige in the philosophical schools. But it has poisoned the reason of Europe, and even in these days intelligent men, otherwise richly endowed, are attacked by its venom. Many minds are wholly corrupted. They have no principles left in virtue of what they call progress; that which is true today may be false tomorrow. They have no longer a single fixed point, and their reason, being truly uprooted, vacillates between an assertion and its contrary and incessantly contradicts itself, while firmly believing in its own fidelity. Intellectual corruption is not the same in all sophists; but we are acquainted with several, regarded as oracles by a considerable portion of the unbelieving world, in whom reason appears to be totally overthrown.

How are such minds to be cured?

I know of but two remedies: humility and the sincere love of truth. Contempt of truth is the characteristic of the sophist, and it is usually the fruit of moral and intellectual egotism — that is, of pride in its highest degree.

The leader of contemporary sophistry himself warns us that the soul must strip itself of all love for being, truth, justice, and God, in order to arrive at confounding being and nonbeing. Listen to the profound teaching of these words:

> The formula, "Being and non-being are identical" appears
> so great a paradox that reason can scarcely regard it in a

serious light. Doubtless no great effort of the mind is necessary to render the assertion, that being and non-being
are the same thing, ridiculous, nor to deduce absurdities
in its application. For instance, it may be maintained as
a consequence of this principle, that it is the same thing
whether my house, my goods, the air I breathe, this city,
the sun, justice, the soul, God, are or are not.... In fact,
philosophy is precisely that doctrine which teaches man
to free himself from a multitude of special ends and points
of view, and renders him independent of everything, so
that it is absolutely indifferent to him whether things are
or are not.[57]

Hegel agrees then with us; the absolute indifference of the
soul with respect to all things is, in his eyes as it is in ours, the
source or nourishment of sophistry. Let this detestable source,
then, be dried up, and sophistry will disappear. Let this deadly
indifference be replaced by the vivifying love of truth, justice,
and goodness; reason will then recover its uprightness, and the
soul, quitting the cloudy abyss where it is struggling, will soar
once again to the pure, serene regions of light.

---

[57] Georg Wilhelm Friedrich Hegel, *Oeuvres*, bk. 6.

9

∞

Unbelief and Natural Religion

Sophistry, skepticism, and materialism are all radical forms of infidelity that attack reason as directly as they attack faith; that is to say, they aim at the total ruin of the moral man. We will again quote Father Gratry, who says:

> We have frequently repeated, after Plato, Leibniz, and others, that the mind of man may follow two contrary tendencies, by the one raising itself toward being, toward God; by the other, sinking toward nothingness; one is followed by philosophers, the other by sophists. Traces of these two tendencies are to be found in all ages; it is an intellectual imitation of the life or death of souls according as they ascend toward God, or depart from him of their own free will.[58]

The infidelity that has been described in the preceding chapters is the act of minds that, by a free and secret choice, descend toward nothingness and plunge themselves into darkness. No Christian age has ever witnessed so many souls given over to

[58] Auguste Joseph Alphonse Gratry, *Logique*, bk. 1, 124–125.

this spirit of darkness as the present. Let not earnest men, who have retained some vigor, some moral uprightness, whether they are believers or unbelievers, deceive themselves. Reason is in peril. In the midst of the astonishing material progress that this century realizes every day, and to which we give our willing admiration — reason, good sense, that something that is the support and necessary safeguard of society, is visibly lowered; the moral standard of men's minds has sunk in a manner that would alarm us, did we not hope in the invincible power of the Christian Faith.

How is it that the best among rationalists, those who join us in our struggles against sophists, obstinately reject this Faith, without which our civilization would soon sink into the abject grossness of materialism? How is it that learned men, who recognize a personal God infinitely good and infinitely wise, all powerful and free, Creator of the world — how is it that they reject all positive intervention of this God in the government of the human race, that they deny the miraculous and supernatural order, understand not that marvelous and, if I may be permitted to call it so, that *natural* effusion of infinite goodness in the Incarnation of Jesus Christ? We must endeavor to clear up this moral mystery.

From the moment men admit miracles, they are no longer infidels, and in our European society they are very near being Christians. Now, is it conceivable that a learned man, whose mind is not corrupted, should recognize a personal and free God, the Master of the universe, and yet deny Him the power of acting in the world as He pleases, according to the dictates of His wisdom and the inspirations of His love? Droz, who had been an infidel for a great part of his life, passes the following judgment on this incomprehensible prejudice:

Infidels have one fixed idea. They will have it that miracles are impossible. When I was but a Deist, I recognized
the absurdity of those who pretended to impose limits on
Divine Power. I will add that this age is too enlightened
for the prejudice which refuses to admit miracles to sub-
sist. The day will come when it will be a consequence of
this simple evident truth: God is an Infinite Being.[59]

Nevertheless, this prejudice, so manifestly contrary to reason,
still maintains its ground.

We remarked, when relating the conversion of the philosopher Justin, that in the early ages of Christianity pagans who
were learned and anxious to discover truth, generally admitted
the Christian Faith from the moment that the idea of the true
God, the Creator of the world, had fully taken possession of their
understanding. The religion of Jesus Christ, with its mysteries,
its institutions, and its practices, appeared to the generous and
grateful souls of these men a consequence and in some sort a
natural application of the idea of a God infinitely perfect, who
is rather the Father than the Master of the human race. The
knowledge of God and of His relations with the world led straight
to the belief in the Incarnation of the Word and in all the ineffable inventions of the love of the Savior of men.[60] There is not

---

[59] Droz, *Aveux d'un Philosophe Chrétien*, 79.

[60] "The Sacrament of the Eucharist," says Madame Swetchine,
"is the noblest expression of a love which can brook no limit,
no separation, no obstacle. By this adorable Sacrament we feel
the presence of God in ourselves, his intimate union, not only
with the spirit, but also with the flesh and blood. The love of
God, Almighty as himself, could go no farther, but thus far it
could go, and in mercy God has stopped only at its extreme

a single pagan philosopher mentioned in the early ages of the Church who rejected the Christian Faith after having accepted the true notion of God. Why is it otherwise in our days? How is it that we see earnest minds admit the natural, while they reject the supernatural part of the Christian Creed? This depends on certain moral dispositions.

After St. Augustine had studied in the school of Plato, he recovered himself nobly; he rose to things appertaining to the intelligible world, and found once more the spiritual and perfect God, who is the light of the world. But the Platonists had not instructed him in the true relations between God and the created universe; they did not know them. Still, in their school he had formed a sufficiently pure idea of God, although it was incomplete and undefined. In this state he saw no difficulty in believing in the Word of whom Christianity speaks, but he could not understand the mystery of the Incarnation of the Word. And why did his mind recoil before this mystery?

He tells us himself it was because he was governed by a pride that hindered him from recognizing and confessing the weakness, the failings, and the moral miseries from which his soul was suffering.[61] When St. Augustine saw himself as he really was, with all the humiliations and all the necessities of his nature, then he understood the benefit of the Incarnation of the Word, and Jesus Christ appeared to him as the necessary Restorer of our fallen nature.

---

limits.... The reality of our Lord's presence in the Holy Eucharist emanates almost necessarily from redemption, as the supreme consequence and highest development of infinite love. The Eucharist is the natural effect of a supernatural charity." Françoise Swetchine, *Méditations et Prières*, 212–213.

[61] Augustine, *Confessions* 7, 20.

Is it not possible that many rationalists are retained in unbelief by the same causes that retained St. Augustine? "You *will not* come to me," said the Word Incarnate Himself to the Jews who rejected him.[62]

The true root of unbelief is the will.

It is pride, it is sensuality, it is egotism in some shape or other that hinders the will from turning toward Jesus Christ and fixing in sincerity the eye of the understanding on this adorable form. "How can you believe," said the Savior to the Pharisees, who were proud of their vain wisdom, "how can you believe, who receive glory from one another, and the glory which is from God alone you do not seek?"[63] And once more: "Men loved darkness rather than the light, for their works were evil."[64]

Human nature is still the same. St. Paul said that the Cross was a stumbling block to the Jews and foolishness to the Gentiles. For God, the Master of the world, to lower Himself, for the love of men, even to die upon a Cross, was, in the eyes, of egotism, an unspeakable absurdity.

When men do not love, how can they understand what love is? When men refer everything to themselves, how can they comprehend the generous and admirable folly of devotion and sacrifice? The Cross of Jesus Christ has exalted human nature. It has become to all civilized nations the symbol of honor and of glory; and nevertheless it remains a stumbling block and foolishness to infidels. When will they surmount the narrow boundaries of that egotism in which they waste away in sterile and delusive self-enjoyment? When will they comprehend that if we, who are

---

[62] John 5:40.
[63] John 5:44.
[64] John 3:19.

evil, can give our life to save one of our brethren, God, who is Infinite Goodness, can empty Himself, according to the expression of St. Paul, take the form of a servant, and die upon a Cross, out of love for His children and to save them?[65] A pure, devoted, humble soul has nothing to oppose to the Christian Faith but beholds in it the most touching and at the same time the most magnificent effusion of the love of God.

Rationalists, I well know, hide their unbelief under fair pretexts. Reason, they say, must not abdicate its sway; reason has prerogatives that it may not renounce. In Christians, they say, reason abdicates by submitting to a power foreign to itself and by accepting mysteries that it cannot understand on the authority of that power.

I wish to believe that men are sincere when they speak thus, but we are so ingenious in deceiving ourselves when the sacrifice of some passion is in question. Ask Droz, Augustine Thierry, Maine de Biran, or any other of the numerous infidels who returned to the Faith, whether they sacrificed one single prerogative of reason in submitting to the authority of the Church; they will answer that they had certainly to sacrifice prejudices and passions, but that on becoming Christians they did but yield full obedience to reason.

Why, then, speak of the abdication of reason, and of a power foreign to reason? Is God a stranger to reason? We Catholics bow before the authority of the Church, because we regard her as the representative and permanent organ of Jesus Christ, the Word made flesh. We believe this not blindly, not lightly, but because the proofs that establish it are evident to the eyes of reason. Faith is finite reason. Obeying infinite reason, or the

---

[65] Phil. 2:5–8.

Word of God, in all things: What can be more just? What more worthy of us?

We admit doctrines, it is true, that transcend reason and that reason can only half understand, but we accept them on the testimony of an authority whose title cannot be disputed. Besides, in things of the purely natural order, the human mind meets with obscurities, with unfathomable mysteries; why, then, should it take offense at mysteries of the supernatural order?

Jules Simon, one of the leaders of spiritualistic rationalism, speaks eloquently of the mysteries of the natural order, but condemns absolutely, in the name of reason, the mysteries of Christianity. This philosopher sees an essential difference between the incomprehensible and mystery in the Christian sense of the word. These are the incredible words that he has written on the subject in the first edition of his book, *La Religion Naturelle*:

> If, in this explanation of the incomprehensible, propositions are enunciated which are not proved, which do not convey a precise meaning to the mind, and *which imply contradiction in terms, this new doctrine is that which properly constitutes mystery.* This doctrine is not only incomprehensible; besides this characteristic it has three others: it is affirmed without being demonstrated; it is not intelligible in its enunciation; it contains a formal contradiction.[66]

All this is false, absolutely false, and in direct opposition to all the teaching of Catholic theology. Christian mysteries are all demonstrated; not in themselves, doubtless, but in revelation, whose existence is verified by reason with an evidence that defies objection; all are intelligible in their enunciation, and no one

[66] Simon, *La Religion Naturelle*, 233–234.

has ever been able to discover the slightest contradiction in a single dogma of Christianity.

Jules Simon knows nothing of our great theologians, who, nevertheless, deserve to be consulted by every earnest philosopher. He knows not that a science exists infinitely higher than the petty philosophy with which rationalism seeks to nourish superior minds, and that this science, which is called theology, consists precisely in the explanation of all those mysteries of which he speaks so lightly. But at least he knows Leibniz, for he has borrowed largely from him.

Now, Leibniz establishes clearly that:

- The Christian mysteries are not contradictory.

- They do not contradict reason.

- They are not contrary to any truth evidently recognized by reason.

- Their enunciation presents a sufficiently intelligible meaning to the mind.

- In short, all objections opposed to them may be solved.

"That which is contrary to mysteries in us," says Leibniz, "is not reason, or the natural light, or the natural sequence of truths; it is corruption, it is error or prejudice, it is darkness."[67] This is what that great man thought of the contradictions that erring minds imagine they have discovered in the mysteries of Christianity.

Let people cease to set the prerogatives and dignity of human reason against the Christian Faith. We believe on good evidence; our faith has nothing in common with credulity. Joubert well observes:

---

[67] Leibniz, *Discours de la Conformité de la Foi Avec la Raison*, no. 61.

Unbelief and Natural Religion

There is a great difference between credulity and faith; one is a natural defect of the mind, the other is a virtue; the first comes from our extreme weakness, the second has a mild and praiseworthy docility for its principle, quite compatible with strength, and which is even highly favorable to strength.[68]

This docility, whence faith springs, is not contrary to our dignity; it is contrary only to our pride. "Let us be men with men," says Joubert once more, "but before God let us be always children; for, in fact, we are but children in his eyes."[69] Dignity, in whatever way we understand it, can only lose by that self-sufficiency that affects to depend on self alone and refuses to bow before the Gospel. "When a man has rebelled against the Gospel," says Madame Swetchine, "he has given himself a master, and that is himself; a master who prepares the way for many more by a continual descent."

Faith is no more opposed to the freedom of reason than to its dignity; as we have already said, it is only contrary to the libertinism of reason. "Why," observes Madame Swetchine,

should not faith bind our understanding as morality binds our actions? Do we cease to be free because we are virtuous? Why should we cease to be free because we are believers? Does not true liberty always exercise itself in a given space? Does it not require a center to attract it, and a basis for its support?[70]

---

[68] Joseph Joubert, *Pensées* 2, 26.
[69] Ibid.
[70] Françoise Swetchine, *De la Vérité du Christianisme*, 85.

10

∞

How Souls Become Unbelievers

I believe that I have now pointed out the chief causes of infidelity. These causes, as I have shown, are many and diverse, but infidelity depends far more on the will and on a certain moral state of the soul than on the understanding. Faith is an act of the understanding, since its object is the revealed truth of God. But in order that the understanding may give its assent to divine truth and firmly adhere to it, the intervention of the will is necessary, and under the inspiration of the grace of God, the will intervenes freely. This grace is refused to none. Faith is free; therefore, it is meritorious; faith is a virtue, and virtue, as a moral act, presupposes freedom.

Man is free to choose between faith and unbelief in the same way that he is free to choose between good and evil, on condition of bearing the responsibility of his choice. We are free to adhere or not to adhere to revealed truth

  • first, because even in things that are evident, it depends on us whether we will turn away the eyes of our understanding from the light that enlightens all things — whether we will arrest the spring of our mind, give it a false direction or even corrupt it

* secondly, because the principal object of faith is not self-evident, but is obscure

"All religion is in the same plane: light is always mingled with obscurity; and why? In order that faith may be a virtue."[71]

This mingling of light and darkness is the necessary condition of this present life, because it is a life of probation; the full day will dawn only when trial shall have ceased.

Ignorance itself, which is one of the commonest sources of infidelity, is often the result of an evil-disposed will. In such case ignorance is culpable, and its guilt is greater or less, according as it is more or less willful. How can we excuse the levity, the dissipation, the indifference in which most unbelievers live, and whence their ignorance of religion proceeds? Are not reasonable beings bound to seek seriously and sincerely the knowledge of the truth?

Moral indifference, the ordinary source of religious ignorance, is capable of leading to every degree of degradation and ruin. When a mind is infected by it, it rarely stops at the rejection of Christianity, but almost always descends to the denial or corruption of the fundamental principles of natural religion; generally, it becomes materialistic and believes only in sensible realities.

Materialism, which is the lowest degree of moral and intellectual degradation, is the most frequent result of indifference in religious matters.

Skepticism, which is the supreme impotence of reason, often depends on a moral condition similar to that which engenders

[71] Joubert, *Pensées* 2, 89.

and nourishes materialism. In certain minds of high intelligence, eager for truth, it may spring from a senseless pride that has had a cruel fall. People flatter themselves that they can remove the limits of reason; they want to be able to see the truth without clouds, and when these clouds, which they believed themselves able to disperse, continually reappear, they grow angry, and end by denying the light because of the shadows that they themselves cast upon it. This is the despair of disappointed pride.

But there is a malady of the soul still more difficult to cure than skepticism or materialism, and it is that condition of intellectual corruption that is called sophistry. We have seen this frightful and fatal malady, which destroys many highly gifted minds. It is useless to seek to convince sophists that they are in error. They will not understand you; they contradict themselves at every step, while they maintain with imperturbable assurance that they never contradict themselves and that they constantly obey reason. They are minds that literally see everything crosswise, and it is impossible to reason with them. "If thy eye be clear," says the Gospel, "thy whole body shall be lightsome; but if thy eye be evil, thy whole body shall be darksome."[72]

The intellectual eye of sophists is evil. Simplicity and clearness must be restored to it; otherwise they cannot receive the light, or they receive it imperfectly. How can this be done? Only by changing the soul in its inmost depths. Let them yield less to egotism; let them love truth more; let their will be simple and just, and their understanding will promptly recover that uprightness that is the condition of true enlightenment.

The greatest obstacle to the Christian Faith is egotism; egotism of the senses, or sensuality; egotism of the mind, or pride;

[72] Matt. 6:22–23.

egotism in every form. We have each of us daily to struggle against this egotism, which shuts out innumerable souls from the light of Faith. If unbelievers, of whatever kind, were animated by a generous love of truth, if they showed that they were ready to embrace it at the price of any sacrifice, they would soon become Christians.

Their will, recovering its rectitude and its moral energy, would turn the eye of the understanding in the right direction and would confirm the understanding in its adhesion to recognized truth. Doubtless we may hesitate even in the face of known truth. But such hesitation is a culpable weakness, and if the will be pure and vigorous, it will not hesitate. Moreover, God will sustain it, because it will be humble and suppliant as it becomes every created will to be.

See this young man of twenty. He has been baptized into the Church of God and has received the divine seed of faith in the sacrament of regeneration. This blessed seed has germinated under the breath of the Holy Spirit and by the culture it has received from the pious solicitude of a Christian family. This young man has made his First Communion, and he has been marked in the sacrament of Confirmation with the seal of Christian manhood.

But now he believes no longer. The Christian life of his soul has disappeared. Faith appears to be wholly extinct within him. He goes so far as even to affect pity for the belief that in his tender years he shared with his mother. He parades a supreme contempt for the teaching of the Church of Jesus Christ. He is astonished that defenders of such teaching can still be found. He is inclined to regard the defenders of the Faith of his childhood as hypocrites, seeking to make their profit out of the ignorance and credulity of the simple. What can have happened to work such a revolution in this youthful mind? If we ask him, he will probably tell us what are the new sources of light whence he has drawn decisive proofs against that old Faith that for nineteen centuries has held captive the loftiest intellects and reigned over the noblest and the purest wills. What has this contemptuous youth seen of the Faith of Bossuet, of Leibniz, of Joseph Görres, of Lacordaire, of Ozanam, of so many eminent men who in our days have adorned and still adorn philosophy, literature, criticism, science?

Hear him: he has scrutinized everything, examined everything by the torch of pure and independent reason. The Catholic Creed cannot sustain for a moment the examination of serious criticism. Philosophy, history, science, agree to condemn it.... What composure! What assurance! What proud, triumphant judgments! But these lofty affirmations, these pompous maxims cannot impose on anyone who has had experience of men and things; such a one easily discovers behind the clatter of pretensions and empty phrases the true history of this poor soul. It is this:

This young man, who so proudly condemns Catholic belief, has examined nothing for himself; he has had neither the leisure nor the will to do so. He has read none of the great works of the Christian apologists; he has not even opened a detailed and scientific exposition of the dogmas that the Church teaches. He condemns Christianity on hearsay with the lightest and blindest faith that can be imagined. His morals being already tainted, doubt entered his soul the first time he heard a contemptuous word spoken with regard to the Faith that had enlightened his tender years; he gave ear to the word of the tempter, which met with a sympathetic and ready echo in a heart already degraded, or on the eve of becoming so.

Unbelief

Doubt having penetrated his soul and disturbed its serenity, he sought not to conquer it. On the contrary, he acted so as to encourage it and with the secret desire of beholding its perfect triumph over the ruins of an austere faith. He let loose his sensual passions, or at least contenting himself with avoiding gross excess, he did but half restrain them. He fed his understanding with writings hostile to Catholicism and would read only such books and journals as calumniated the Church in her dogma, her worship, her history, her present life, in all her manifestations. These writings, in which ignorance rivals hate, are henceforth his sole light, his sole authority in religious questions. He blindly repeats the sentences he finds in them, imagining perhaps that he is judging the teaching of faith with entire intellectual independence.

Poor young man! Your affected independence of reason will deceive only children; any serious observer will tell you how you have descended all the steps of the ladder of doubt and infidelity. He will give you the history of your moral and intellectual falls, and placing his finger on the wounds of your heart, as well as on the wounds of your understanding, he will force you to confess, if you are sincere, that reason and science have no part in your condition, and that your unbelief is the fruit of weakness and decay of every kind.

Do not deceive yourself: infidelity is not an elevation, but a degradation. It is a fall, a moral and intellectual decline, and this decline in a young man who has been educated in the Christian Faith is usually brought about by the ruin of more faculties than one.

Some young men fall into infidelity in consequence of manifold low and degrading actions that have extinguished their moral life. Many, thank God, descend not thus far; they stop themselves on the sad incline. They lose the Faith by hostile teaching, by irreligious reading, by conversation with indifferent or adverse companions, by the very atmosphere of infidelity that surrounds them. But although their soul may have undergone many falls, the moral life still animates it. La Bruyère said: "I would fain see a man who is sober, moderate, chaste, equitable, declare that there is no God; he would at least speak disinterestedly; but such a man is not to be found."[73]

For my part, I would fain see a young man who is chaste, modest, humble, seriously instructed in Christian doctrine, declare, that the Faith which he received from his mother the Catholic Church is without foundation: hitherto I have never met with such a young man.

But what I have often seen, what we see every day, is this: men of ripe intellect, after years of wandering, return to the Faith and to the practices that it imposes, acknowledging and declaring, in all humility, that their unbelief was but the fruit of vanity, ignorance, or passion. It is a fact of daily observation that men regain the summits of faith by the pure and persevering love of truth and virtue, as they descend into the abyss of infidelity by pursuing a contrary path. A pure and humble soul, loving truth and justice, opens of itself to the light of faith; and the holier it is, the higher in the moral order, the greater its knowledge of God and of itself, the deeper and more lively will be its faith. Faith grows in direct proportion to the purity and moral light of the soul. This is a fact attested by the whole history of Christianity. I will conclude by recommending this fact to the consideration of all sincere men.

---

[73] La Bruyère, *Caractères* 16.

Unbelief

The cure of unbelief will obviously be found in serious reflection on the preceding truths, and in earnest prayer for light and grace:

> I wished, and understanding was given me; and I called upon God, and the spirit of wisdom came upon me: And I preferred her before kingdoms and thrones, and esteemed riches nothing in comparison of her.... Now all good things came to me together with her, and innumerable riches through her hands.... For she is an infinite treasure to men! which they that use, become friends of God.[74]

Ask, with the confidence of the blind man of Jericho: "Lord, that I may see."[75]

---

[74] Wisd. 7:7–8, 11, 14.
[75] Luke 18:41.

∞

Bibliography

Aristotle. *Nicomachean Ethics.*

Augustine. *Confessions.*

Bossuet, Jacques-Bénigne. *Traité de la Concupiscence.*

Brownson, Henry F. *Faith and Science; or, How Revelation Agrees with Reason, and Assists It.*

Droz, François-Xavier-Joseph. *Aveux d'un Philosophe Chrétien.*

Gibbons, James. *The Faith of Our Fathers: Being a Plain Exposition and Vindication of the Church Founded by Our Lord Jesus Christ.*

Gratry, Auguste Joseph Alphonse. *Logique.*

———. *Une Étude sur la Sophistique Contemporaine.*

Hegel, Georg Wilhelm Friedrich. *Oeuvres.*

Joubert, Joseph. *Pensées.*

Jouffroy, Théodore. *Mélanges Philosophiques.*

Justin. *Dialogue with Trypho.*

La Bruyère, Jean de. *Caractères.*

Unbelief

Labbé, Philippe. *Sacrosancta Concilia ad Regiam Editionem Exacta.*

Leibniz, Gottfried Wilhelm. *Discours de la Conformité de la Foi Avec la Raison.*

Maine de Biran, Pierre. *Journal Intime.*

Pascal, Blaise. *Pensées.*

Plato. *Phaedo.*

—————. *Republic.*

Rohrbacher, René François. *De la Grâce et de la Nature.*

Simon, Jules. *La Religion Naturelle.*

Suárez, Francisco. *De Fide.*

Swetchine, Françoise. *De la Vérité du Christianisme.*

—————. *Méditations et Prières.*

—————. *Pensées.*

Tacitus, Cornelius. *Annals.*

Thomas Aquinas. *Summa Theologica.*

Biographical Note

∞

Fr. Nicolas J. Laforet

(1823–1872)

Born at Graide, Belgium, on January 23, 1823, Nicolas Joseph Laforet completed the regular theological course at the seminary of Namur before entering the University of Louvain, where he applied himself especially to the study of Oriental languages, Holy Scripture, and philosophy.

In 1848, he was appointed to the chair of moral philosophy at the university and, the same year, received a doctorate in theology. Two years later he became president of the College du Pape. There he founded schools of civil engineering, industry, and mines, as well as a new literary and pedagogical school, the Justus Lipsius Institute.

Throughout his academic career there, Laforet's example and advice were a constant encouragement for both professors and students.

Laforet was a member of the Royal Academy of Belgium and of the Roman Academy of the Catholic Religion. Besides a great number of articles, especially in the *Revue catholique*, Laforet's works include numerous scholarly and popular books of theology, history, biography, and apologetics, as well as a history of philosophy, of which only the first volume on ancient philosophy was completed before he died at Louvain on January 26, 1872.

Sophia Institute

Sophia Institute is a nonprofit institution that seeks to nurture the spiritual, moral, and cultural life of souls and to spread the Gospel of Christ in conformity with the authentic teachings of the Roman Catholic Church.

Sophia Institute Press fulfills this mission by offering translations, reprints, and new publications that afford readers a rich source of the enduring wisdom of mankind.

Sophia Institute also operates two popular online Catholic resources: CrisisMagazine.com and CatholicExchange.com.

Crisis Magazine provides insightful cultural analysis that arms readers with the arguments necessary for navigating the ideological and theological minefields of the day. *Catholic Exchange* provides world news from a Catholic perspective as well as daily devotionals and articles that will help you to grow in holiness and live a life consistent with the teachings of the Church.

In 2013, Sophia Institute launched Sophia Institute for Teachers to renew and rebuild Catholic culture through service to Catholic education. With the goal of nurturing the spiritual, moral, and cultural life of souls, and an abiding respect for the role and work of teachers, we strive to provide materials and programs that are at once enlightening to the mind and ennobling to the heart; faithful and complete, as well as useful and practical.

Sophia Institute gratefully recognizes the Solidarity Association for preserving and encouraging the growth of our apostolate over the course of many years. Without their generous and timely support, this book would not be in your hands.

www.SophiaInstitute.com
www.CatholicExchange.com
www.CrisisMagazine.com
www.SophiaInstituteforTeachers.org

Sophia Institute Press® is a registered trademark of Sophia Institute.
Sophia Institute is a tax-exempt institution as defined by the
Internal Revenue Code, Section 501(c)(3). Tax I.D. 22-2548708.